Needlelace

Needlelace
Designs and Techniques
Classic and Contemporary

Catherine Barley

B.T. Batsford Ltd · London

Typeset by Goodfellow & Egan Ltd, Cambridge
Printed in Singapore

Published by
B.T. Batsford Ltd
4 Fitzhardinge Street
London W1H 0AH

A catalogue record for this book is available from the
British Library

ISBN 0 7134 6810 6

The frontispiece shows a woodcarving of a Venetian Gros
Point cravat by Grinling Gibbons, from the Devonshire
Collection at Chatsworth House, Derbyshire

To Nenia, my teacher and friend, whom I can never repay for giving so generously, over the years, of her time, knowledge, enthusiasm and encouragement. Thank you for enhancing my life.

A thing of beauty is a joy for ever:
Its loveliness increases; it will never
Pass into nothingness . . .

Keats

Contents

Acknowledgements   8
Introduction   9

Part 1: Traditional Techniques   11

   Gros Point de Venise   13
   Hollie Point   40
   Point de Gaze   52
   Scrolls   76
   Classic Needlelace: Some Antique Samples   103

Part 2: Bridal Accessories   113

   Tissue Purse with Flower   117
   Coronet and Shoe Rosettes   125

Part 3: Contemporary Projects   135

   Three-Dimensional Strawberries   137
   Peapods with Butterfly   142
   The Promise of Spring   150
   The Gardenia   154
   Swan with Raised Wings   159

Part 4: Pattern Section   163

Book Suppliers   173
Sources of Information   175
Index   176

Acknowledgements

My grateful thanks to students and friends who have helped in the production of this book, namely Myriam Jonkers for working some of the samples to test that my instructions were easy to follow; Nina Devereux, Marge Quinn and Marie Laurie for allowing me to photograph and illustrate their work; Marjorie Crump for the tea-cosy design; Doreen Holmes for reproducing my Hollie Point designs on her computer; Dr Spriggs for permission to photograph lace from the Spriggs Collection now housed at Rougemont House, Exeter. My thanks also to Mr P. Day, Keeper of Collections at Chatsworth House, Derbyshire, and Mrs Christine Thompson, seamstress at the house, for allowing my husband to photograph the Grinling Gibbons wood carving and the lace collection for reproduction. To Joan Ford for the flower arrangements, Jennifer O'Leary for her wedding dress, Agnes Stevens for teaching me some of the Zele techniques and Barbara Hirst for introducing me to stumpwork.

I should like to extend my thanks also to Ron Head for his patience and expertise in developing and printing my black and white photographs, and finally to my husband Roy for taking the colour photographs and for redrawing all my patterns and diagrams.

Introduction

I used to make and teach bobbin lace long before I had ever heard of needlelace. In 1978 I enrolled at Windsor and Maidenhead College for a two-year City and Guilds Creative Textiles course, the tutor being none other than Nenia Lovesey. Like so many lace teachers I had no qualifications and, as this course covered both bobbin and needlelace, it seemed to me to be a step in the right direction. Hence my introduction to this beautiful form of lace, which I hasten to add, I did not enjoy at all to begin with: I much preferred my lovely bobbins. My stitches were uneven, and I could not get the wretched lace off the backing material. I had a lot to learn and, as for so many of those taking the City and Guilds Creative Studies lacemaking course today, it was something that had to be covered in the syllabus, so I had to make a sample.

My first sample was not very impressive, but I could see the potential, and I was amazed to learn that with the same basic loop or detached buttonhole stitch it was possible to produce a lace which was known as Gros Point de Venise, but for all the world looked as though it could have been carved from ivory, or a lace as fine and delicate as gossamer, called Point de Gaze. At this stage in my reluctant pursuit of knowledge, I knew nothing of, nor had even heard of, Hollie Point, Youghal, Halas or Zele, never mind the many other types of needlelace.

This book is not intended for the complete beginner but for those with a basic knowledge of needlelace. It is divided into four sections, the first covering a selection of the various classic types of needlelace, namely Gros Point de Venise, Hollie Point and Point de Gaze. A small sample of each type of lace is given, with detailed working instructions and diagrams, enabling the worker also to recognise and identify the prominent characteristics of these laces.

The stitches have not all been grouped together in one section of the book, but have been covered at the beginning of each project. Diagrams only have been given for the stitches most frequently used, and which I feel confident the worker will already be familiar with, whilst diagrams and full instructions have been included for the lesser-known stitches and techniques. I suggest that a small sample is worked of each stitch required for a particular project before commencing, that is of course if the lacemaker is not already familiar with the technique. The samples follow a progressive course, enabling the worker to transfer the knowledge gained from the previous piece of work. Repeated use of a technique or stitch is one sure way towards achieving perfection, and the more often a technique is called upon, the more likely it is to be remembered.

The second section covers projects for bridal accessories, whilst the third covers contemporary projects that incorporate the techniques mastered in the execution of the traditional samples. I realise that it is not possible to please everyone, but have done my best by including several types of needlelace, both classic and contemporary. Lacemakers who have advanced beyond the contemporary pieces might perhaps like to try their hand at some of the classic projects. Some of the scrolls, wheels and shading in the Point de Gaze section might inspire the worker to select one or two samples that they have particularly enjoyed working and arrange them into a design of their own for a fan leaf, collar or maybe a wedding veil. This may sound a daunting task, but the individual pieces are quite small, and needlelace is very portable. It is surprising how quickly they mount up.

The fourth section contains patterns for lacemakers to work on their own. Several of them are combinations of samples already covered in the first section of the book, and are intended to help those who claim that they cannot design, illustrating how easy it is to make an original pattern by adapting one or maybe two designs that are particularly appealing. Sometimes all that is needed is simply a mirror image. Also covered in this section are Hollie Point samples that can be mounted into a baby's bonnet as a christening gift.

Stumpwork is at present enjoying a revival, and I feel that embroiderers could learn a great deal from the techniques used by the needlelace maker, in the execution of the detached buttonhole stitch required to make the tiny articles of clothing in stumpwork. It seems such a natural extension of needlelace, and one that I particularly enjoy, but unfortunately space does not allow it to be included in this book.

Making and teaching needlelace is an occupation that has enriched my life, taking me to many countries, where I have met a variety of knowledgeable and interesting people and made many very good friends. It has given me an immense amount of pleasure and fulfilment and it is my hope that others will gain as much from it as I have.

PART 1

Traditional Techniques

Gros Point de Venise

Gros Point de Venise came into being during the early part of the seventeenth century and was made until the middle of the eighteenth century. It has been said by many to resemble carved ivory, but made of the finest of threads. Heavily raised and richly adorned with many minute buttonholed loops and picots, it was held in high esteem, much sought after and regarded as a status symbol. There are several other types of Venetian needlelaces, such as Rosepoint and Point de Neige, which are similarly ornate but not as heavily raised as the Gros Point, and also flat laces known as Point plat and Coralline.

A gentleman by the name of Grinling Gibbons, born in Rotterdam in 1648, was not a lacemaker but a woodcarver, whom Horace Walpole described in 1798 as 'an original genius, a citizen of nature'. Many examples of his work can be seen in churches, stately homes and museums. He was a man who was appreciative of the many beautiful things that surrounded him, and Venetian Gros Point lace has been cleverly incorporated into many examples of his work. The cravat displayed at Chatsworth House, Derbyshire, is an outstanding example of his skill and workmanship, and it is hard to imagine that this was once a solid piece of wood. (See frontispiece.)

Stitches

Very few filling stitches are to be found in Gros Point de Venise. The most commonly used are corded Brussels, with veins and diamonds, a little double Brussels, small areas of pea stitch and of course the Gros Point diamonds. The outstanding feature of this needlelace is the heavily raised cordonnette, decorated with a variety of buttonholed loops, picots and couronnes.

Corded Brussels

See diagram 1.

Double Brussels

See diagram 2.

Pea Stitch

See diagram 3.

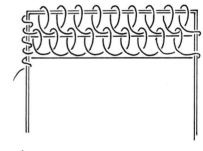

Diagram 1

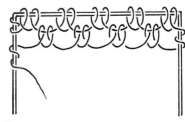

Diagram 2

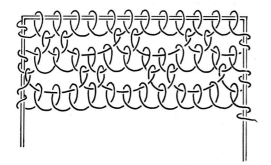

Diagram 3

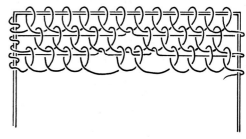

Diagram 6

Small Diamonds

Work corded Brussels to the area where you wish to make your first diamond.

Row 1. Take your cord across from one side of the work to the other, but whip into the stitch where you want the first hole to be. (See diagram 4.)

Row 2. Return by working one stitch into each loop formed in the previous row, *but miss*

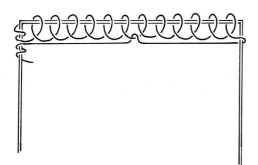

Diagram 4

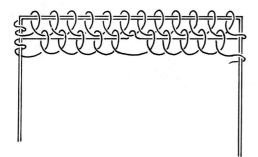

Diagram 5

the loop that you slipped into in the row above. Now you have made your first hole. (Diagram 5)

Row 3. You now need to make one hole immediately to the left of this hole and one to the right, forming a pyramid. Take the thread across the work, but this time you will need to make three consecutive whips, one into the loop before the hole, one into the hole, and one after the hole.

Row 4. Once again work into each loop of the previous row until you reach the first loop that you whipped into (to the left or to the right of the first hole, depending on whether you are left or right handed). Miss this loop, work *two* stitches into the hole above, then miss the next loop, which again is the one you whipped into. Remember that two stitches make one loop, so to make up the loop missed in the previous row, it is necessary to make two stitches. (Diagram 6)

Row 5. Make three whips in this row also: one into the hole, one between the two stitches, and one into the next hole. Take the cord the rest of the way across. (Diagram 7)

1 Venetian Gros Point sample from the Spriggs Collection now housed at Rougemont House, Exeter

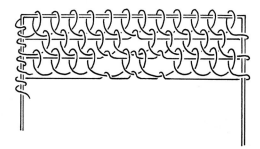

Diagram 7

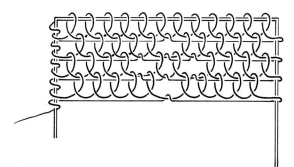

Diagram 8

Row 6. Work one stitch into every loop of the previous row, work *two* stitches into the first hole, miss the next loop, then *two* stitches into the next hole. Complete to the end of the row. (Diagram 8)

Row 7. You now have a pyramid shape and need to make the last hole in the centre to complete the diamond. Take your thread across once more, whipping into the central hole. (Diagram 8)

Row 8. Work back, one stitch into every loop of the previous row, and *two* stitches into the final hole.

Nine Hole Diamonds

Now that you have worked a four hole diamond, try working a nine hole one from the chart. (Diagram 9)

Gros Point Diamonds

Try working a sample using No. 20 crochet cotton. You will find it easier to count the stitches. Having worked a small diamond, you will find it fairly simple to follow the graph illustration to work these larger diamonds, which are so frequently seen in Venetian Gros Point.

Make a foundation row of evenly spaced stitches.

Row 1. Take the working thread across from one side of the work to the other, but * whip into the first loop, miss eight loops and repeat from * to the end of the row.

Row 2. * Miss one loop (the one that you whipped into), make eight stitches, repeat from * to the end of the row.

Row 3. Take the thread across, but whip into the hole and the loop after the hole. * Miss five loops, whip into the loop before the hole, the hole itself, and the loop after the hole (three consecutive whips). Repeat from * to the end. (Diagram 10)

Row 4. * Work two stitches into the hole, miss one loop, work five stitches, miss one loop. Repeat from * to the end of the row. (Diagram 10)

It is important to remember to think one row ahead. In other words, when laying your thread across, remember to whip into the stitch where

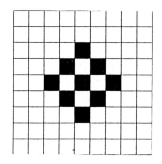

Diagram 9

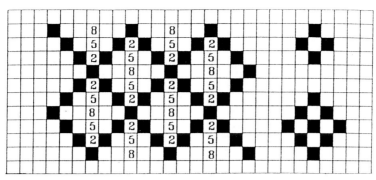

Diagram 10

you wish to make a hole, and having made it, remember to whip into it in the following row.

Continue working from the chart now that you have your pattern set. It will be far less confusing than the written word.

Veins

Work corded Brussels to the position of the first row of veins, finishing with a buttonhole row, which is worked from left to right.

Row 1. Take the cord back across the work by whipping into alternate loops across the complete row, from right to left. (Diagram 11)

Row 2. Work Point d'Espagne (also known as Hollie stitch or English stitch) in alternate loops, but this time work it into the loop that you *did not* whip into. Pass the needle under the cord and hold the thread from the eye of the needle, wrapping it under the needle from left to right and *under* the working thread from the previous stitch. Repeat to the end of the row. (Diagram 12)

Row 3. Whip back into every loop across to the other side of the work.

Row 4. Work two single Brussels stitches into each space. (Diagram 13)

Tip. The following is a useful way of increasing or decreasing on a curved area of work, where necessary, in the middle of a row. To increase, work three stitches into the occasional loop, and to decrease work only one stitch into the loop. Use your own judgement as to where you think this should be.

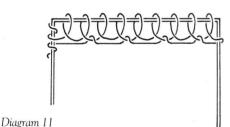

Diagram 11

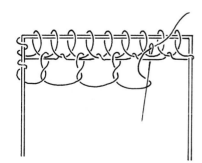

Diagram 12

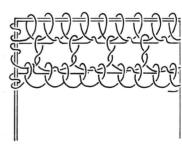

Diagram 13

17

Pattern 1
Venetian Gros Point Sample

This small sample of Gros Point could be mounted on silk and used for a purse, or mirror imaged for a belt or box lid.

Materials Required

No. 20 crochet cotton in ecru
Gütermann 100/3 silk ecru
Ringstick or size 14 knitting needle
Tapestry needle or fine crochet hook

A pillow is not essential as all fillings stitches can be worked without one, but it is nevertheless far easier to do the raised work with the aid of a pillow. This enables the many threads required to be manipulated with the left hand, leaving the right hand free to work the filling stitches. Use whichever method you feel most comfortable with.

Couching

Tips before you start

1. Try to start from the centre of the design when couching, and work towards the outside. It should then be possible to complete the couching without any joins.

2. Always make sure your cordonnet is kept taut whilst being couched down, in other words there should be no slack in it. This will make for a better tension when working the filling stitches, and it will be easier to work an evenly spaced foundation row. If the cordonnet is slack it will pull away when you work your first row of stitches, resulting in the edge of the design resembling a polygon instead of maintaining its original elegant curve.

Gros Point sample designed and worked by the author. (Pattern 1)

Pattern 1

Diagram 14

3. A thimble will probably be required when raising the cordonnette, to avoid having a sore finger. You may also find a small pair of pliers quite useful!

Tack the pattern and architect's linen to the calico. Take a length of No. 20 crochet cotton (approx. 2½ metres) and fold it in half to form a loop. Thread a sharp sewing needle with strong tacking cotton, and knot the end. Start at **A** in diagram 14, bringing the needle up from the back of the work through all layers of fabric, pattern, architect's linen and, finally, through the loop of crochet cotton. Take your needle over the doubled length of crochet cotton and back down into the same hole. Continue to work couching stitches approximately 2–3 mm. (⅛ in.) apart. Remember it is essential to keep the cordonnet taut.

Continue round this central trefoil shape, back to **A**. Divide the threads at **A** and take one thread only through the loop formed at the beginning. (This will be referred to from now on as 'join'.) A crochet hook or crewel needle is ideal for this purpose.

Pick up the remaining thread and continue to

couch both threads to **B**. Divide the threads and take one on to **C** and join. Return to **D**, whipping (oversewing) to the first thread.

Take the single thread from **D** to **E**, join and return to **D**, whipping to the thread already couched as you go, and back to **B**. Continue round to **F** and repeat as for the first half of the design, until you reach **G**.

Divide the threads at **G** and take a single thread on to **A**, join, and return to **G**. Put in a couple of extra stitches, secure at the back of the work and fasten off. Cut off both cordonnet threads so that the cut ends butt up together.

Working the Fillings

Tips before you start

1. Before commencing your first row of filling stitches in a particular area, study it for a moment or two. If necessary, draw a light pencil line across a copy of the pattern and fill in the whole of the area in this manner. It may then become apparent that the direction you have chosen to work your filling is not necessarily the best way. You may have left yourself some rather small and extremely

2 Venetian Gros Point sample designed and worked by the author

difficult areas to work. If so, try again from a different angle.

2. Prick in your four hole diamonds with a needle or pin. This will help to centralise them and also to give a visual 'plan', which helps tremendously and is far better than working at random.

3. Keep a spare copy of your original pattern, as you may find this useful to refer to when you have completed all your filling stitches. Often it is difficult to decide whether an area comes in front of or behind another at this stage, and the original drawing may therefore prove to be very useful.

Stage 1

Area B

When working this section of the design it is far easier to work the rows of corded Brussels vertically instead of horizontally, avoiding the necessity of lining up the final rows of the three sections. It is not always possible to do this, as some stitches have to be worked horizontally across the design, but this will be covered later in the book.

First lightly score the pattern down the centre with your ballpoint needle or scissors, and score several more lines back to area **D**

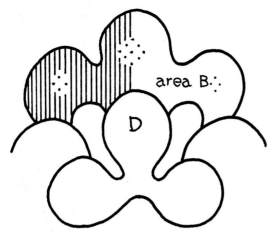

Diagram 15

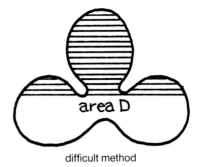

difficult method

Diagram 16a

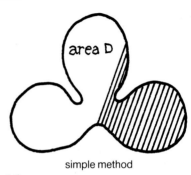

simple method

Diagram 16b

(diagram 15). This will give you the angle and position of the first row to be worked, and will help to position the diamonds in the correct place when you come to work them. Remember to prick them in with your needle. Work a four hole diamond either side and a nine hole diamond in the centre section.

Area D

Now that you have mastered the Gros Point diamonds by first working a sample in No. 20 crochet cotton, you will feel far more confident at tackling them in this pattern. Normally one would probably start at the top of this area, working as far as possible before starting the left-hand side of the trefoil shape, then the right, endeavouring to keep the pattern correct to meet with the central area. As you can appreciate, this would be extremely difficult to do, but not impossible! I suggest, therefore, that you work the diamonds diagonally across this area, starting as indicated. This is a far easier way of keeping the pattern correct. (See diagrams 16a and 16b, and photograph 3.)

Areas A

Refer to diagram 17. These two areas are worked in pea stitch, but you could substitute

double Brussels. Work the first row from **a–b** as indicated in diagram 18. Working the rows in this direction makes it easier to keep the continuity of the pattern, when working into the small area at the base of the shape, than if the rows were worked horizontally.

Areas C

Finally work areas **C** in corded Brussels with open veins, as indicated (diagram 19).

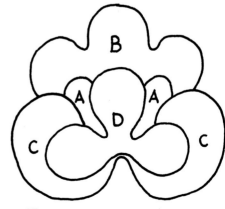

Diagram 17

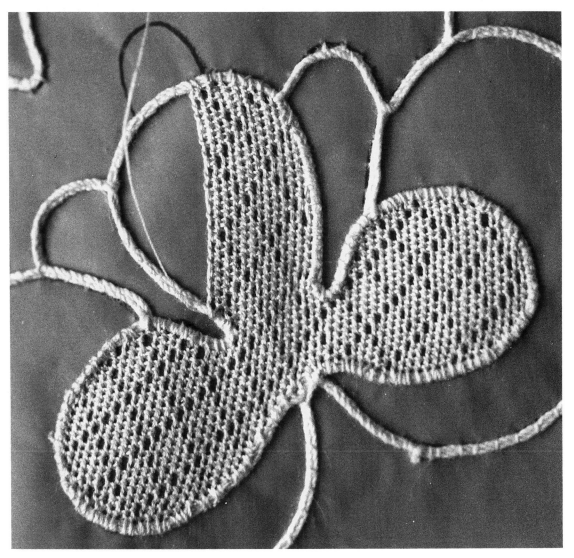

3 Detail of Gros Point diamonds

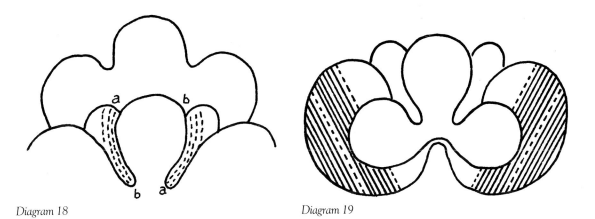

Diagram 18

Diagram 19

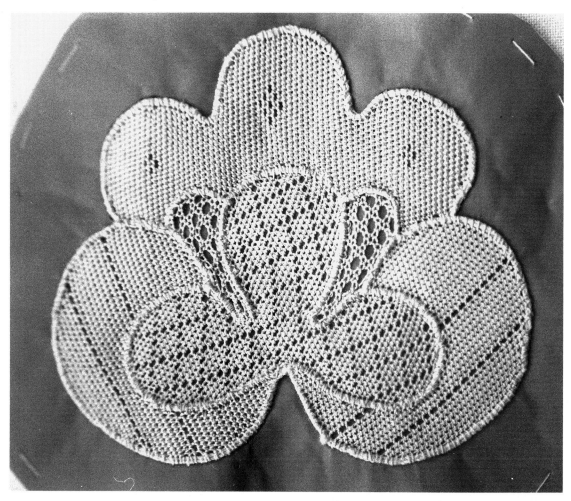

4 Venetian Gros Point sample with all areas filled, ready for raising

Working the cordonnette

Tips before you start

1. Always be conscious of the length of your working thread. Try to project ahead to a difficult area of the work, e.g. a tight 'hairpin bend' or picot, and try to renew your thread before negotiating this area, ensuring you have sufficient thread to complete it.

2. Try using a fine sharp needle instead of a ballpoint when working the buttonholed loops along the cordonnette, as the needle tends to separate the threads when it is passed three times into the same hole, making a gap

between them. There is also a danger that the loop may break.

3. First study the design and decide which areas come to the front and which come from behind another area. When I look at the design, I see the small areas worked in pea stitch and marked **A** in diagram 17 being the farthest away. To create the three-dimensional effect required, this area would need to be raised the least, and would therefore be worked first.

4. Area **B** comes from behind area **C**, so this would be the next to be worked. Area **C** comes in front of **B**, but from behind **D**, so would be

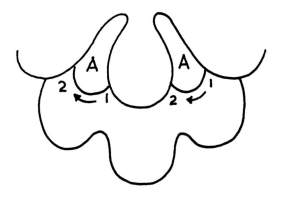

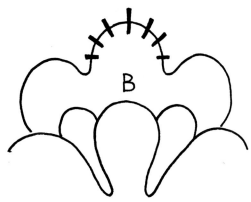

Diagram 20

Diagram 22

the third area. Area **D**, finally coming to the front of the design, would be the last to be worked, and the most highly raised.

There are two different methods to work the raising of the cordonnette. The first is gradually to build up the threads, laying them in one at a time, and the second is to use the 'trace' method. Both these methods will be explained as required.

Areas A (Diagram 20)

Take a short length of No. 20 crochet cotton and fold it in half to form a loop. Thread your needle with 100/3 silk to work the buttonhole stitches, and secure this working thread by running it underneath the couching stitches, bringing it out at point 1 in diagram 20. Bring your needle through the loop formed by folding the crochet cotton in half, and work buttonhole stitches over these two threads, with the edge of the stitch on the outside of the curve. You should of course include the

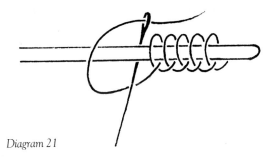

Diagram 21

background of filling stitches that you have already worked. Work from right to left to manipulate the large number of threads that you will have to hold with your left hand during the next stage of the work. This is assuming that you are right handed. If not, then work from left to right. Leave a small loop extending and work three or four stitches to ensure a firm beginning, then place your needle into the loop of crochet cotton and pull the two loose ends until the loop disappears. This will close up the loop, and placing the needle in it will prevent it from twisting up (diagram 21). Work across to point 2 in diagram 20. Cut off one of the lengths of crochet cotton and leave the working thread along with the remaining strand of crochet cotton. These threads will be picked up and used later.

Stage 2

Area B

The tops of the three areas to be raised have first to be prepared by working the 'fil de trace', which is the quicker method of building up the threads and forms a crescent or croissant shape. (Diagram 22)

Take a sharp needle threaded with strong sewing cotton doubled (preferably a colour contrasting with that of your work) and with a knot in the end. Bring the needle through from the back of the work (through the calico,

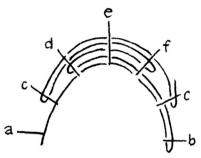

Diagram 23

pattern and architect's linen) and make a large
stitch over the work. Take the needle through
to the back of the work. The length of the
stitch will determine the depth of the raising,
so make the largest stitch at the top of the area
first, then make three more stitches either side
of it, graduating down to approximately 2 mm.
(1/16 in.). Secure thread at the back of the work
(diagram 22). The two small stitches are often
difficult to locate, so the use of a contrasting

colour for these stitches does help. Prepare left
and right sides in the same way.

Take a tapestry needle threaded with a long
length of No. 20 crochet cotton and run this
round under all the stitches from **a–b** (diagram
23). Take the thread back over **b** and under the
other stitches back to **d**. Work back and forth
under the top three stitches (**d**, **e** and **f**) until
approximately half the depth of these stitches
has been packed with thread, then continue on
to **c**, working back and forth from **c–c**. When
these stitches are *almost* fully packed, continue
right round all stitches from **a–b**. If the top
three stitches are not fully packed at this stage,
continue to work back and forth from **a–b** until
they are. Any length of thread remaining when
you have completed the padding can be left, as
this will be picked up with the extra threads
that are to be laid in during the next stage of
the work. (See photograph 5.)

5 Detail: building up the 'trace'

Adaptation of a Dover design incorporating Venetian
Gros Point techniques, worked by the author.

The stitches are packed so tightly with threads
that ridges are formed by the 'trace' stitches,
which have to be covered by laying in extra
threads, making the finished work so smooth
that it resembles satin. To achieve this effect,
the buttonhole stitches must be so close
together that the threads beneath do not show
through.

You will find it far easier to work the
cordonnette if you now pin the work to a
pillow, and place a chopstick or knitting
needle between the pillow and the work to act
as a lifting stick. This will form a ridge, making
it much easier to manoeuvre your needle.

Take a length of crochet cotton doubled, and
start at point 3 in diagram 24, working from

right to left. Make one or two stitches with the
100/3 silk over these threads. The 'trace'
stitches will of course be removed when the
work is completed, so it is essential that you
make sure you pick up the cordonnet and the

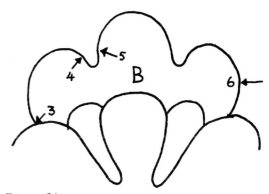

Diagram 24

filling stitches underneath. If you only pick up the padding, then it will not be attached to the work when it is removed from its backing.

Building up the threads

Cut a short length of No. 20 crochet cotton (approx. 15 cm.) and lay in this new thread by placing it on the inside edge of the cordonnette, leaving a short tail extending to the right and the remainder of the thread to the left. Work two or three stitches, then add a second thread. Continue to add threads in this manner.

The work will look rather like a paintbrush at this stage, with maybe seven or eight new threads projecting to your right. (See photograph 6.) When the first thread has been worked over by approximately 2 cm. (¾ in.) and you feel that it is secure, pull the short end (which will be to the right) and watch the bundle of threads lying to the left, to see which

one moves. Pick up this thread in your left hand and gently pull it until the tail end on the right just disappears under the stitches worked. Be careful; it is very easy to pull too hard and pull the thread right out, especially if your buttonhole stitches are a little loose.

There is no reason to hurry in making these new threads disappear; gently ease each one through when you feel it is safe to do so. It is amazing how tightly they will pack down, and you may have as many as ten or even twenty new threads in the bundle – it is for you to decide just how raised you wish the work to be. Remember the depth of your 'trace' stitches will have determined this to a large extent, and you will have to continue laying in extra threads until you have sufficient to lay over the padding already prepared, making a smooth surface over the ridges that will have been formed by the 'trace' stitches. If you find you have small gaps between your stitches, lift the bundle of threads with your left hand and ease

6 Detail: laying in extra threads

them to the right. This will close up any small gaps.

Continue working round this area, holding the bundle of threads in your left hand (or right if you are left handed), guiding them round the curve until you reach point 4 in diagram 24. Check the length of your working thread at this stage. If it does not appear to be long enough to work round this tight bend, run in a new thread now. It is far more difficult to make a neat join with the edge of the buttonhole stitch on top of the work, especially in such a confined space. If you have run in a new thread, work one or two stitches.

Negotiating a tight bend

It is necessary to turn the edge of the buttonhole stitch, which has until now been along the outside edge of the work. Sometimes these hairpin bends in Gros Point can be very tight, with the two sides of the bend almost touching each other, making it practically impossible to work them in the customary manner. By pulling the needle vertically (towards the ceiling), instead of horizontally (towards your body), the edge of the buttonhole stitch will gradually turn towards the top of the work, making it far easier to manipulate the bundle of threads around these tight bends. Keep pulling the working thread towards the ceiling until you reach point 5 in diagram 24, then reverse the process by pulling the needle towards you again. The stitch will gradually revert back to its normal position.

Proceed round all three padded areas until you reach point 6, where it will be necessary to begin reducing the number of threads used for the padding. Examine the bundle of threads, select the shortest one, and cut it off on the diagonal and as close as possible to the work. Be careful not to cut your working thread! Make one or two stitches, then cut off another. Always select a thread from the bottom of the bundle if possible, as they will be less likely to show. Reduce these threads down to two or

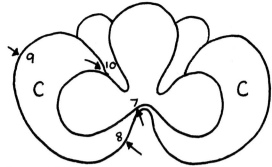

Diagram 25

three and leave them; they will be picked up when working the next area.

Save all your odd lengths of crochet cotton, as some of them will be long enough for future use.

Stage 3

Area C

Make the 'trace' stitches and build up as for area **B**. Start at point 7 (diagram 25) with a doubled length of No. 20 crochet cotton and gradually build up the threads by laying them in one at a time as before, but this time incorporating a 'trefoil' edge (photograph 7). This edge is worked at the same time as the cordonnette.

Single buttonholed loop

Work the cordonnette to point 8 in diagram 25, which will be the position of your first loop. (Remember to lay in your extra threads.)

1. Take the needle back anything from 10–13 stitches, and slip in between the next two stitches, forming a loop. It will vary according to the tension of the individual lacemaker, and also the size that you wish to make your loops. It is always a good idea to change to a fine sharp needle for this stage of the work.

2. Take the needle back to the left and slip between the last two stitches worked. You will now have two threads forming the loops.

7 Detail of trefoil loops

3. Take the needle back again to the right and slip once more into the same space. You will now have three threads forming the loop. Place your needle into this large loop and gently ease the working thread to make sure that all three threads are the same size, then proceed to buttonhole stitch over them until the loop is full (diagram 26). Continue to work the cordonnette with 10–13 stitches more, remembering at the same time to add your extra threads.

Diagram 26

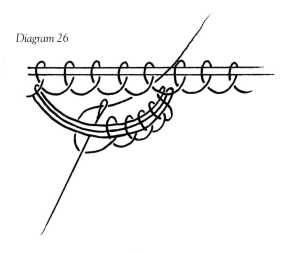

30

Casket designed and worked by Marge Quinn. The inspiration for this project came from a stumpwork casket in the Burrell Collection, and the needlelace design on the doors was taken from the gates of the town hall at Warrington, Lancs.

Trefoil loops

4. Repeat the process for the first loop, slipping into the cordonnette loop *next* to the first loop buttonholed (not the same one). Repeat until you have three threads forming a second loop.

5. Proceed to buttonhole stitch over this second loop, but only halfway this time. (Diagram 27)

6. Take the working thread back to the centre of the first loop and repeat the sequence again,

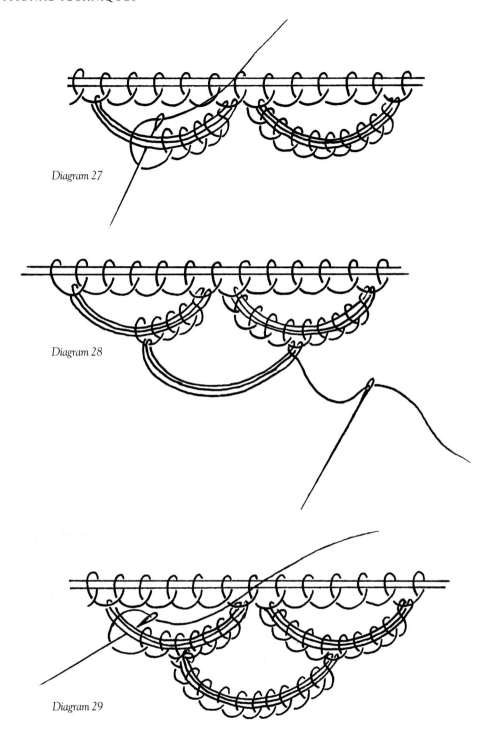

Diagram 27

Diagram 28

Diagram 29

making three threads to form the third loop. (Diagram 28)

7. Finally buttonhole stitch over the whole of the third loop and continue on to finish the

remaining half of the second loop. (Diagram 29)

These groups can be positioned next to each other, or with a space between each trefoil.

They could be made incorporating tiny loop picots or Venetian picots, which can be positioned in a variety of ways.

Proceed to work round this area, adding your new threads and remembering also to keep an eye on the length of your working thread whilst working these buttonholed loops. Make sure that it is long enough to complete the whole loop and possibly two or three stitches after the loop. It is obviously far easier to run in a new thread when working the stitches between, than it would be if it were to run out whilst actually working the loop.

Work round to point 9 in diagram 25, which is approximately three-quarters of the way round area **C**. Reduce the number of threads to two by the time you have reached point 10. These will be picked up at a later stage. Work the other side in the same way, picking up and working into the cordonnette the threads that were left from areas **A** and **B**.

Stage 4

Area D

Prepare the padding using the 'trace' method as before, for all three sections of this area.

1. Start at 11, using the two threads left from the area **C** cordonnette, and gradually build up the threads again, working round to 12, where you will turn the edge of the buttonhole stitch to the top of the work as before (diagram 30). At the same time work a Venetian picot every seventh stitch, with zigzag loop between each one. (See photograph 2.)

Venetian picots

Working from right to left, work the cordonnette to the position of the first picot.

1. Work a buttonhole stitch but, before pulling it tight, place a pin in the loop, positioning it as far from the cordonnette as length of picot required. Stick the pin into the

pillow, with the working thread to the right of the pin. There will always be a small loop at the end of these picots where the pin has been, so the finer the pin you use, the better.

2. Take the working thread round the pin and make the first buttonhole stitch by working over only one of the three threads. This will make a stitch into the end of the loop, which prevents the remainder of the stitches slipping off the end of the picot. (Diagram 31)

3. Work the remainder of the stitches back over all three threads towards the cordonnette. Continue to buttonhole stitch along the cordonnette, but do not remove the pin until you have worked a couple of stitches after completion of the picot. (Diagram 32)

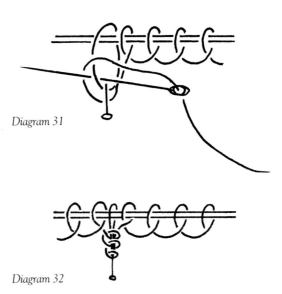

Diagram 30

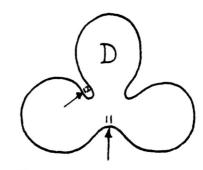

Diagram 31

Diagram 32

Zigzag loops

Work cordonnette as usual, at the same time incorporating evenly spaced Venetian picots.

1. Work two Venetian picots evenly spaced, then one stitch past the second picot. Now take your needle back to the right, just past the first picot, and make a loop. Repeat as before to make a buttonholed loop over three threads, but buttonhole stitch only halfway across the loop. (Diagram 33)

2. Turn the needle away from the body and pick up a small section of the cordonnette, attaching the loop to the inside edge. (Diagram 34.)

3. Turn the work 180° (or work the stitches with the needle away from you) and continue to buttonhole stitch the remaining half of the loop, keeping the edge of the buttonhole stitch on the same side as the first half of the loop. The second half will of course be worked from left to right instead of from right to left, as for the first half. When the remainder of the loop has been worked, turn the work to its original position and continue. You will now have a cordonnette with Venetian picots along the outside edge and zigzag loops across the top (diagram 35). Remember to continue laying in the extra threads, and lengthen the size of the loop to correspond with the depth of raising. (See photograph 2.)

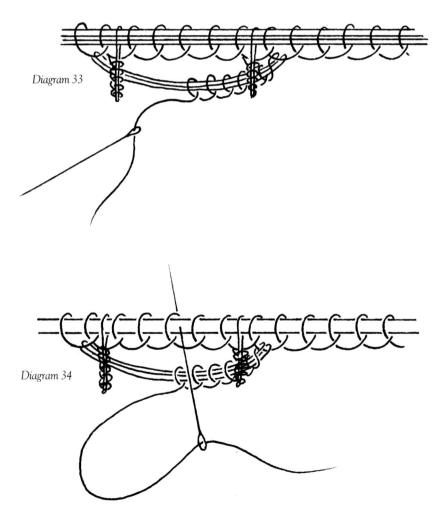

Diagram 33

Diagram 34

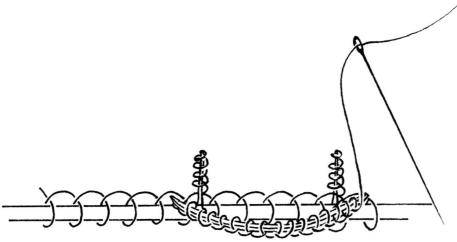

Diagram 35

As the raised area begins to narrow, start to reduce the number of threads in preparation for the tight bend that will be worked next. Remember to begin pulling the working thread vertically (towards the ceiling) to start the edge of the buttonhole stitch turning towards the top, and make sure that your thread is long enough to work completely round the bend.

Repeat the whole process for the remaining sections, and complete, reducing the threads down to nil.

Couronnes

There are several ways of working couronnes, but for this particular piece we shall incorporate two of them. They can be worked on a ring stick or knitting needle and applied to the lace when it has been finally removed from its backing; worked directly onto the lace before it is removed; or worked using the 'trace' method and applied after completion of the lace. I find the trace method the simplest, whether it be for really thick couronnes with picots and loops, which are extremely difficult to work in the hand, or quite tiny ones that prove equally difficult to handle.

Applied couronnes

Determine the size you wish your couronne to be and use the trace method, making either four or six stitches in the form of a circle instead of a crescent shape. If the couronne is to be a tiny one, four stitches will be sufficient, but six may be required for a large size. The length of the stitches will again determine the thickness of the couronne. These stitches can be worked on a small area round the outside of your sample, as they will be removed and applied to the work when it has been completed (diagrams 36a and 36b). Take a length of No. 20 crochet cotton and run it round and under the trace stitches until they are tightly packed with the crochet cotton. Cut off what is not required.

Take a long length of No. 100/3 silk, run the thread underneath the trace stitches and round once or twice to secure it, then proceed to buttonhole stitch round the ring. The couronne could be plain or decorated in a variety of ways. I have worked Venetian picots at regular intervals round the edge, but buttonholed loops could be used, with or without Venetian picots or tiny single loop picots. (Diagram 37)

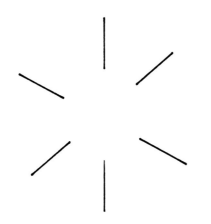

Diagram 36a

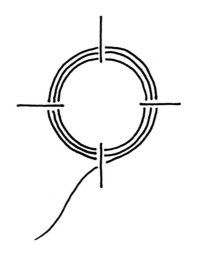

Diagram 36b

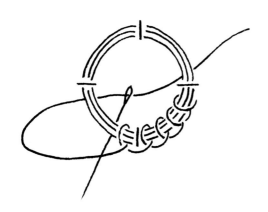

Diagram 37

To join the couronne

When you have worked completely round the couronne, join the ring by taking your needle into the loop made by the first two stitches. Leave the remainder of the working thread attached, as this is used to stab stitch the couronne into position when the sample is removed from its backing. The trace stitches are cut by separating the layers of fabric and snipping the stitches between, just as you would after completion of the sample.

Threaded couronnes

These couronnes look as though they have somehow been threaded onto the work, and remind me of the bone and wooden Bucks lace bobbins known as trolley bobbins, which had loose rings or 'gingles' that were skilfully turned as part of the bobbin when it was being made. Threaded couronnes may be worked singly, or you may prefer several all the same size, or graduating in size, or decorated with loops and picots. I have worked them with buttonholed loops and Venetian picots either side.

A size 14 knitting needle was used here, but the smallest section of a ring stick could also be used.

1. Take a fine sharp needle and run a very long length of 100/3 silk under the cordonnette stitches, bringing it out to the top of the cordonnette at the position chosen to work the couronne. Work a couple of stitches through the cordonnette to secure the thread.

2. Lay the knitting needle or couronne stick over the top of the completed cordonnette and take the working thread over the knitting needle and through to the underside of the cordonnette. You will need to take the thread round in this fashion at least 20 to 25 times,

8 Detail of the Grinling Gibbons woodcarving shown in the frontispiece

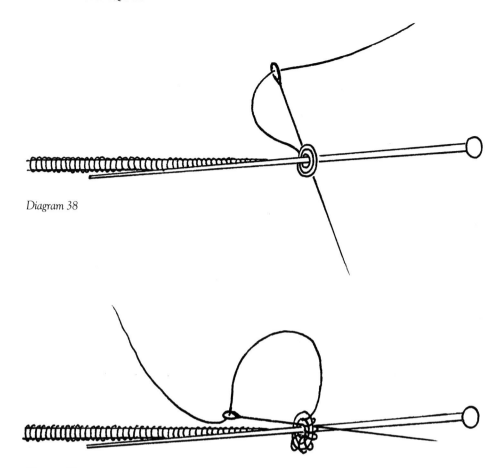

Diagram 38

Diagram 39

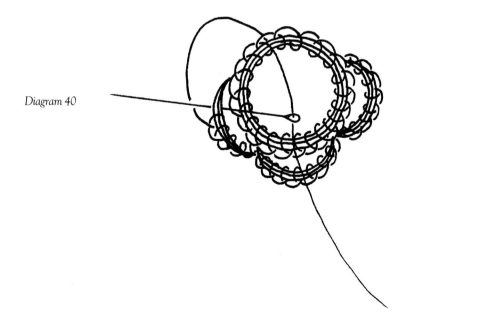

Diagram 40

possibly more, depending on how thick you wish to make the couronne. (Diagram 38)

3. Buttonhole stitch over these threads to form a couronne, working as many stitches as you can with the needle or ring stick still in position. Eventually the loop will become too tight to work and it will be necessary to remove the knitting needle to complete the whole of the loop. (Diagram 39)

4. When the loop is fully worked, pass the needle right through the centre of the cordonnette (not underneath it) from one side to the other. Repeat this process several times

to make sure that the thread is secure, then cut off the remaining thread.

Flower couronnes

Tiny flowers can be made by simply working a couronne with buttonholed loops round the outside edge. Usually these loops are worked at the same time as the buttonhole stitches (as you did for the cordonnette), but I find it far easier to complete the couronne then work round a second time, making the buttonholed loops. Working the loops after completion of the couronne will give a more even distribution. (Diagram 40)

Hollie Point

Hollie Point (or Holy Point) was made from around 1720 until the early part of the nineteenth century and is generally regarded as an English lace. Extremely fine and depicting Biblical symbols, it was almost always used as insertions into baby clothes, either the crown of a bonnet, the front of a christening gown, or perhaps the shoulders of a chemise or jacket. Not surprisingly, samples of this lace were quite small; its patterns were geometric and portrayed symbols such as the Lamb of God, the Tree of Knowledge, the Holy Dove, the Lily of the Annunciation, the Crown of Glory and the Star of Bethlehem. The mortality rate for babies at that time was high, and it is believed that these symbols had meanings such as 'keep this child safe'.

The formation of the pattern is the same as that of the diamonds worked in the previous Venetian Gros Point sample. However, instead of single Brussels, it features Hollie stitch, also known as Point d'Espagne or – in Belgium – English stitch. When I asked Belgian lacemakers why it was so called, they didn't seem to know, but I feel it would be reasonably safe to assume that it was because the lace was generally considered to be English in origin.

The stitch therefore has three different names, each with a different method of execution; basically, however, these are all exactly the same – a buttonhole stitch with an extra twist. The amount of tension applied to the thread, and the direction in which it is worked, will affect the final appearance of the completed stitch. If the thread is pulled tightly, the twist will be pulled along the vertical bar of the stitch, but if less tension is applied, the twist will stay at the bottom of the stitch, giving the appearance of a little knot. It is rather difficult

to unpick, but you may already have discovered this when working the veins in the previous Gros Point sample.

In Belgium the stitch is worked upside down (the reverse way up) and this I find to be the quickest and easiest method, although when it was first shown to me by Agnes Stevens at the English Lace School I have to confess that I found it extremely difficult. However, practice makes perfect!

Stitches

English Stitch (Diagram 41)

This stitch is worked the reverse way up (away from the body). Take the needle under the cord as you would to form a corded Brussels stitch, then hold the thread from the eye of the needle and twist it once anti-clockwise round the tip of the needle. Take the needle *over* the working thread from the previous stitch. If you pull tightly and wiggle the thread from left to

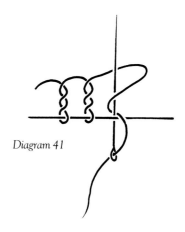

Diagram 41

9 Hollie Point bonnet designed and worked by the
author

right, the twist will slide along the vertical bar,
but if you do not pull as tightly or wiggle the
thread, one twist will stay at the bottom,
giving the appearance of a little knot. This
stitch has a Z-twist and the working thread
passes over the top of the loop.

Point d'Espagne (Diagram 42)

Work this stitch towards the body. Pass the
needle under the cord and hold the thread from
the eye of the needle, wrapping it under the
needle from left to right and *under* the working
thread from the previous stitch. Ease the

working thread to tighten. This stitch also has
a Z-twist but this time the working thread
comes from underneath the stitch.

Diagram 42

41

Hollie Stitch (Diagram 43)

Diagram 43

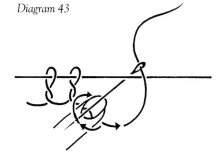

Place the left thumb over the working thread, take the thread in the right hand, over and behind the thumb from right to left, forming a loop. Take the needle behind the cord and through the loop to form the stitch. This method gives an S-twist with the working thread passing over the top of the loop.

10 Hollie Point practice sample worked by Myriam Jonkers using No. 20 crochet cotton

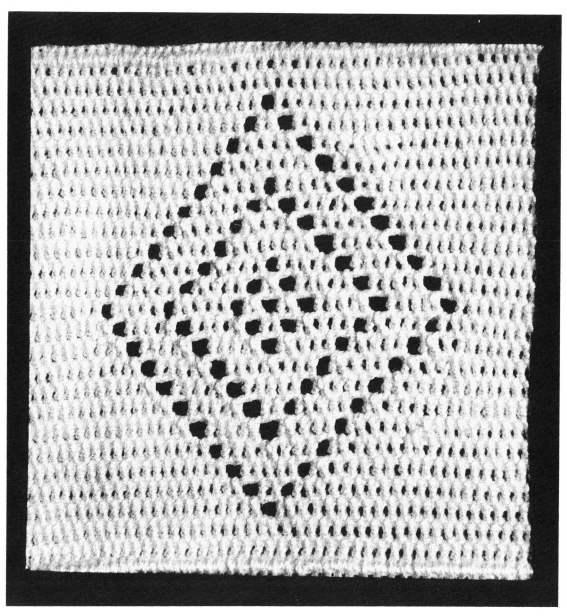

Hollie Point Practice Sample

Try working a sample using No. 20 crochet cotton. (*Do not* attempt this unless you have mastered the Gros Point diamonds described on pp. 16–17.) Couch down a square approximately 6 cm. × 6 cm. (2½ in. × 2½ in.) and try working each of the three methods described, so that you feel confident about the execution of one of them by the time you have completed the sample. This will make for ease of working when you try the sample a second time, using the very fine thread. (Photograph 10)

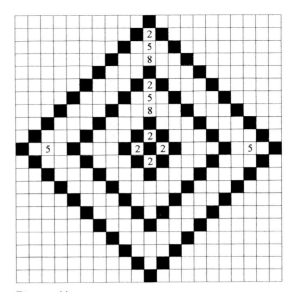

Diagram 44

Materials Required

No. 20 crochet cotton
Ruler

Row 1. Refer to diagram 44. Take the thread across from one side to the other.

Row 2. Work a row of evenly spaced Hollie Point stitches across the complete space.

Row 3. Cord.

Row 4. Work a second row of Hollie Point stitches.

Row 5. Take the cord from one side to the other, but this time slip into the central loop across the row.

Row 6. Work a Hollie stitch into every loop except this central loop. Complete the row by working into every remaining loop. This will give you your first hole, as with the diamonds in the previous sample.

Row 7. Take the cord across the work, but slip into the loop before the hole, the hole itself, and the loop after the hole. Secure the stretched cord to the other side of the work.

Row 8. Work a Hollie Point stitch into every loop except the first loop that you slipped into. Miss this loop, work two stitches into the hole, miss the next loop.

Work the rest of the sample from the chart (diagram 44).

Now that you have worked a sample in thick thread and are confident with both the formation of the stitch and the pattern, you will be ready to try the same sample using the fine thread.

Pattern 2
Hollie Point Insertion

Antique samples of Hollie Point were worked
in linen thread and inserted into garments also
made of fine linen. If you are fortunate enough
to have some old fine linen thread, the finished
result will look more authentic, but the closest
that I was able to get was with No. 120 Copley
Marshall thread used for making Honiton lace.
A Brok 160 cotton thread or Egyptian cotton
No. 120 will give a similar result.

Tips before you start

1. You will find this work rather trying on the
eyes, so I recommend that you use either
dark-blue or green matt adhesive film instead of
architect's linen. The fine white threads do not
show up well against the pale-blue colour of the
linen, which results in very tired eyes.

2. Myriam Jonkers worked this sample and as a
complete beginner found it helped to draw the
rectangle onto millimetre graph paper, to
maintain an even tension, and also to regulate
the spacing on the first row. If you are
experienced you should not find this necessary.

3. When working the first two rows of the
sample, which are *not marked* on pattern 2, it
will help if you can think of them as two rows
of bricks. The first row will be a complete row
of whole bricks, but when you come to work
the second row, lay your first brick with one
half over the first brick in the previous row,
and the other half over the second brick, so
that they alternate. If you continued laying
bricks the complete length of the row, you
would find that you had a space the size of half
a brick at either end. This represents the small
loop referred to in the written instructions to
follow.

Pattern 2

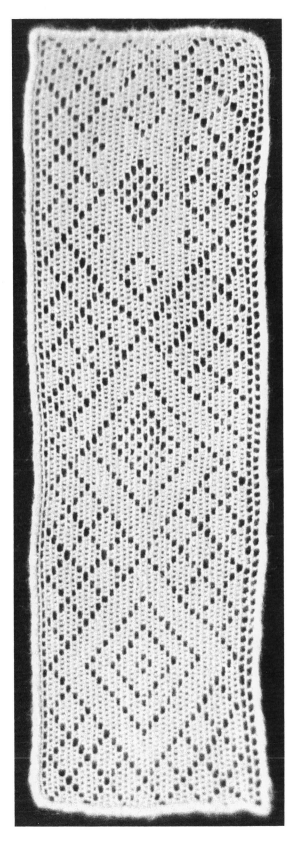

Materials Required

Brok No. 24 cotton for cordonnet
Brok No. 160 or Egyptian Cotton No. 120
Size 15 Fresia sewing needles
Ruler
Dark-blue or green matt adhesive film
Millimetre graph paper (optional)

Each and every one of you will have a different tension, and *it is essential* therefore that you work a small square enabling you to determine your natural tension. It is not possible for me to state the exact size of the square or rectangle to be couched down, as it will be different for each of you. If you have not already done so, try working the practice sample again, this time using the fine thread instead of the No. 20 crochet cotton. You will need to use a very fine needle, otherwise the thread, being so fine itself, will continually come out of the eye. A thick needle will also separate the stitches made in the previous row. I did find the needle rather small and particularly sharp to start with, but I soon became accustomed to this, and eventually was quite happy with it.

Antique samples are sometimes worked across the long length of the work and sometimes across the short length (diagrams 45a and 45b). If there are a large number of holes to be worked immediately one above the other (for example the stem of a lily), it is obviously easier to work the sample across the long length, as you will be working the holes side by side, as for the veins in the Gros Point sample. If only one or two holes have to be worked one above the other, it is possible to work them across the short length. Remember, though, that having made a hole it is necessary to work two stitches into it in the following row to make up the loop that you missed in the previous row. If you don't, there will be too few

11 Hollie Point sample designed by the author and worked by Myriam Jonkers

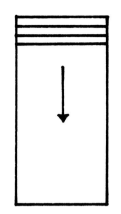

Diagram 45a

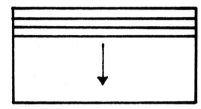

Diagram 45b

taking the needle in from the top of the last stitch, bringing it out underneath the stitch. Continue to work over both threads for several stitches. Cut off one thread, work a few more stitches then cut off the tail end of the other thread. Depending on which of the three methods you have used to make the stitch, you will either take the needle holding the new thread in from the top of the stitch or from underneath, bringing it out on the top. (Diagrams 46 and 47)

Draw a rectangle approximately 18 cm. × 2.5 cm. (7⅛ in. × 1 in.). Couch down three-quarters of one short side and one long side of the rectangle, using Brok No. 24 for your cordonnet (diagram 48). Leave the remaining length of cordonnet until you have worked the foundation row.

Row 1. Work a foundation row of evenly spaced Hollie Point stitches with a space between each large enough to work two stitches into in the following row. Work sufficient stitches to give a total of seventy-

loops in the following row and your pattern will not work out. This is what would happen if you made three holes one on top of the other without making any stitches into the previous hole, so it is essential that both the number of stitches and the tension remain constant.

Joining in a New Thread

Working along the long side of the pattern presents the problem of having to work with longer lengths of thread, which tend to knot frequently or fluff. It is however possible to join in a new thread in the middle of a row. I found it difficult to judge accurately the length of thread needed to complete a row; sometimes I would get almost the whole way across, but not quite, and I did not feel inclined to attempt unpicking three-quarters of a row!

You should have no problem judging the length of thread required for the corded row, but if it runs out in the stitching row, simply leave the old thread and run in a new one by

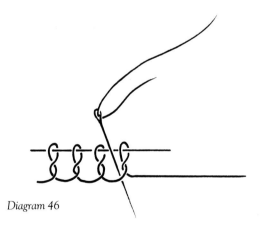

Diagram 46

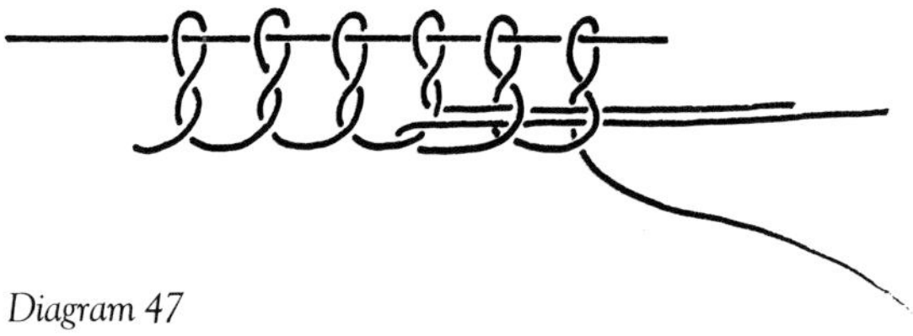

Diagram 47

12 Hollie Point bonnet (English, eighteenth century)

seven spaces. At this stage of the work you can lengthen or shorten your cordonnet, continuing also to couch down three-quarters of the third side (diagram 49). I found it almost impossible to count the large number of stitches across this row, even by counting them as I actually made them. Somehow I always seemed to lose my concentration for one reason or another, but by making two rows of this open edge it was relatively easy to count. This sample is worked across the long side because it is not possible to make seventy-seven holes one on top of the other, which you would need to do if it were worked across the short row.

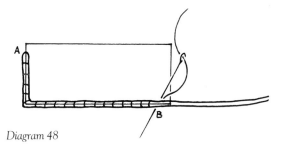

Diagram 48

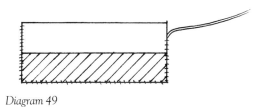

Diagram 49

47

Row 2. Whip back into every hole to the beginning.

Row 3. Work another row of stitches, working one stitch into the centre of each space in the previous row. Think of this as your second row of bricks.

Row 4. Whip back into every hole.

Row 5. *This is the first row shown in pattern 2.* Miss the first loop (which is a small one, and makes the first hole), * work two stitches into each of the next four holes, and one stitch to the right-hand side of the next hole. Make two stitches into each of the next three holes, and one stitch to the left-hand side of the next hole*. Repeat from * to the end. This will give you a row consisting of 18 holes and 17 blocks of eight stitches, as indicated on the chart.

Row 6. Whip into the hole and the loop after the hole. * Miss five loops, make three consecutive whips. Repeat from * to end.

Continue to work from the graph until you have worked exactly half of the pattern. Measure the completed half of the work and couch down sufficient cordonnet to accommodate the other half. It might be prudent to leave the fourth side of the rectangle until you have only a few rows left to complete, as your tension will vary slightly from day to day, and may not be identical to that of the first half. Adjust the cordonnet as required. It is not necessary to work a cordonnette round the completed sample; simply remove it from its backing in the usual way. It is now ready to be inserted into your chosen garment.

Pattern 3
Hollie Point Insertion

This sample has a long stem down the centre, so the simplest way to work it is across the long length of the pattern, working these holes side by side. Make a foundation row of 88 spaces and work two rows of open edge as for the previous sample. The next row is the first row on the chart.

My first experimental sample had no border, and I found it extremely difficult once again to count large numbers of stitches. Eventually I found that by working a small border of diamonds, which was relatively simple, it was quite easy to mark the centre of the border on my graph paper, and also to mark the centre of each of the small pyramid shapes, and relate one to the other, using them as reference points. In this way I did not need continually to count large numbers of stitches, but simply worked one hole immediately to the left of the central hole, then one to the right, or missed two loops then worked three holes, etc. It was then only necessary to count small numbers of stitches, saving much frustration.

I think no further explanation is needed to work this sample. The main requirements are good eyesight, patience and an even tension.

Pattern 3

To Work a Row of Vertical Holes

If you continually try to work one hole above the other without making up the stitches missed in the previous row, obviously your number of stitches across the row will gradually decrease, resulting in the holes becoming larger. It is necessary, as you have already discovered, to keep the number of stitches constant, so work one stitch into the previous hole, but work it close to the left side of the hole. In the following row of stitches (the third hole) again work only one stitch, but this time work it close to the right side of the hole. In other words, work the stitch alternate sides in each row. The row will waver slightly, but this is fine as long as there are only one or two holes.

Circular Samples

The most difficult thing was to get my chosen design in the centre of the circle, because initially I had no idea what size the finished piece of work would be. The first sample of the Holy Dove that I worked was way over to the right, and of course could not be used. However, this did convey the size that it would work up to. I was then able to trace the dove (or photocopy it) from my worked sample and position it in the centre of the circle to be worked for the crown of the bonnet. Another lesson learned: never throw away your mistakes, you can always learn from them!

The Holy Dove

See pattern supplement 1 on p. 164. The horizontal rows of adjacent holes in the tail, wings and undercarriage of the dove are worked exactly the same as for the veins in the Gros Point sample (see p. 17) and the stem of the lily in pattern 3 (i.e. one stitch into every other loop). The shape of the bird would be distorted if they were indicated by missing every other square on the paper, as in the previous Hollie Point patterns.

Designing Your Own Patterns

When designing your own patterns, do not be fooled by thinking that because your design has worked out on graph paper, it will work out in practice.

To centralise one hole within a given space, you must have an odd number of loops, and to have an odd number of loops you must have an even number of stitches.

Study the two diagrams 50 and 51. They both appear to be correct. Diagram 51 is correct, but diagram 50 is not. You will notice that in the final row of diagram 50 a hole is marked in the centre, with two spaces either side. This will not work in practice because there are only five stitches, and five stitches will make four loops. It is not possible to centralise a hole if there are only four loops, as there would be two spaces on one side and only one space on the other side. Not quite as simple as it appears!

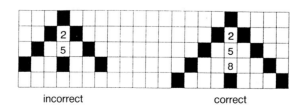

incorrect   correct

Diagram 50   *Diagram 51*

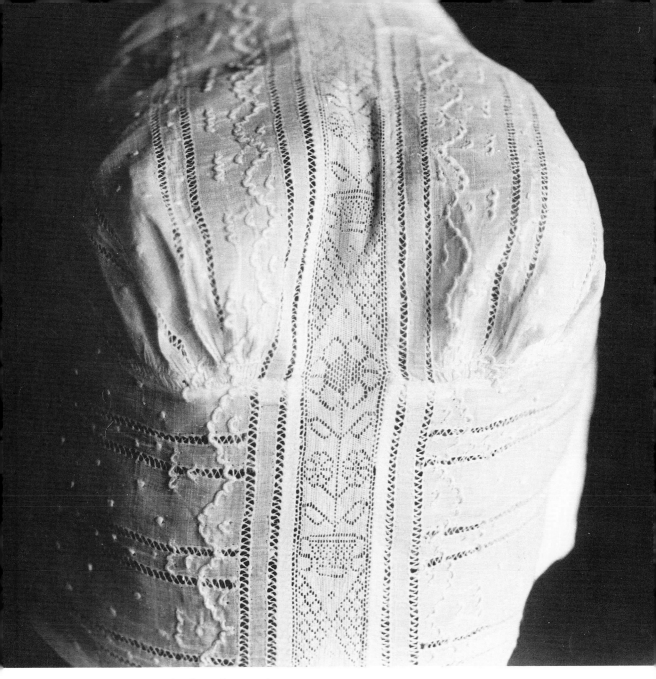

13 Hollie Point bonnet (mid-eighteenth century)

Point de Gaze

Point de Gaze is a needlepoint lace made in Brussels from about the middle of the nineteenth century. Its main feature is its delicate gauzy ground and tiny buttonholed rings, which were used for bud motifs and a variety of fillings. The designs are incredibly beautiful, usually depicting naturalistic sprays of flowers, sometimes with separate layers of petals giving an added dimension.

Students are frequently anxious to learn as many different filling stitches as possible in a very short space of time. I feel it is far better to become proficient at just one or two stitches. Some of the antique samples of Point de Gaze illustrate this point admirably.

So far we have covered Gros Point de Venise and Hollie Point, and all the stitches in these samples have been worked over a cord, making it far easier to regulate the tension. The finer the thread, the more difficult it is to maintain an even tension, and it is this which makes a piece of work outstanding.

This first Point de Gaze pattern is worked to a much larger scale than the antique samples, and therefore requires a thicker thread, but there is no reason why having first worked it in the thicker thread you cannot reduce the flower and use a finer gauge.

14 Brussels Point de Gaze lappet from the Spriggs Collection, now housed at Rougemont House, Exeter

Pattern 4
Point de Gaze Sample

Pattern 4

Materials Required

Brok cotton No. 24 for the cordonnet
Brok cotton No. 100/3 for the filling stitches

Refer to diagram 52. *Do not couch lines not indicated on the diagram.* Start at **A** and proceed round one side of each ring as indicated to **B**, on round the last ring in a figure-of-eight movement and back to **A**, joining each ring where the threads cross, and also the loop made at the beginning.

Continue on to **C**, take a single thread to **D**, return to **C**, and on to **E**. Take a single thread from **E** to **A**, join and return to **E**.

Work on from **E** to **F** and on to **G**. Take a single thread from **G** to **H**, return to **G** and continue on round (joining where lines cross) to **I**. Take a single thread from **I** back up to **F**, join and return to **I**.

Work round the next petal to **J**, and continue round the small petal above, joining to the small petal on the left, and on to **K**. Take a single thread from **K** to **C** and back to **K**, then on to **L**. Take a single thread from **L** to **M** and back to **L**, on to **B**, join and continue to **N**. Take a single thread from **N** to **J**, join and back to **N**, and on to **O**.

Take a single thread from **O** to **P** and back to **O**, then on to **Q**. Take a single thread back to the previous petal, join and return to **Q**. Finish the rest of the flower in the same way, joining where necessary. When you reach **R**, take a single thread to join the first petal and return to **R**. Put in a couple of extra stitches to make sure that the cordonnet is secure, fasten off at the back of the work, then cut off the threads closely. The two ends of the cordonnet threads should butt up together.

Now you have couched the first flower, no further instructions will be given for this procedure. It will be assumed that you are already competent at couching the cordonnet.

Tips before you start

1. Make sure that you have Brok 100/3 and *not* just 100, which is much finer. The 100 has blue lettering on the label, whereas the 100/3 has red lettering, is clearly marked 100/3, and is a thicker gauge.

2. When you are working curved rows, you will find that the radius increases far more quickly; make sure, therefore, that you increase sufficiently at either end of the row. So many workers cannot understand why when they start off with a beautifully even foundation row, they finish with a very uneven tension.

Try to imagine a piece of pastry: the larger you roll it, the thinner it becomes. The same thing happens when you try to make too few stitches cover a larger area. The loops have to become bigger to cover the extra space, resulting in an

15 Point de Gaze flower worked by Myriam Jonkers using Brok 100/3 cotton

Diagram 52

uneven tension. Just as in knitting, it is essential that you increase by sufficient stitches to maintain an even tension and keep the pattern repeat correct.

Filling Stitches

The stitches used are corded Brussels, making four hole diamonds where indicated, and Point d'Espagne. To give the flowers some movement and make them look more natural you will need to learn how to control the rows of stitches, making gentle curves rather than the rigid straight rows that have so far been worked. Nothing is new, you are just going over old ground and reinforcing techniques

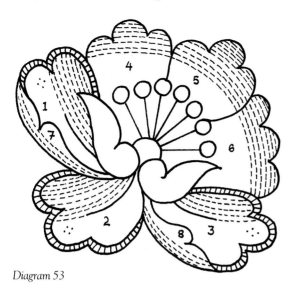

Diagram 53

Refer to pattern 4 on p. 54. The solid line in the centre of the petal indicates the position of an open vein; the four dots indicate a small diamond. First score the pattern with the end of a needle or pair of scissors, extending the length of the open vein. Continue to score lines, maintaining a gentle curve to create the 'cupped' effect, back to the top of the petal (diagram 55). This will give you the position and angle of your first row.

The chances are that your rows will not begin and end quite where you scored them on the pattern; they are meant only as a rough guide. It is not easy to make these curves exactly where you want them, but this will come with experience. Each petal worked will be better than the last, and it may be that you will wish to cut out the filling worked in the first petal, then work it again!

already covered, but using them in a different way.

The bottom three petals are worked with an open edge which is made by working Point d'Espagne (or Hollie stitch), as indicated in diagram 53, with curved rows of corded Brussels to accentuate the cupped petals. An open vein is worked in the centre of each petal and is indicated by a thick line.

Petal 1

Work Point d'Espagne from **A** to **B** (diagram 54), leaving a space between each one large enough to accommodate two stitches in the following row. Work *two* stitches into the same point at **B** to form a V-shape, enabling you to negotiate the bend. Continue on to **C**, making the final stitch an ordinary buttonhole stitch (without a twist), as this stitch needs to be shorter where the area reduces to a wedge shape.

Whip back once into every space, but twice into the V-shape. Keep the working thread slack at this point so as not to distort the shape. This will be referred to as 'open edge' throughout. (Diagram 55)

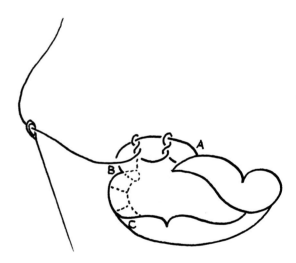

Diagram 54

Diagram 55

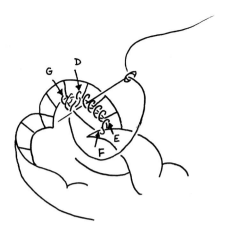

Diagram 56

Row 1. Work single Brussels from **D** to **E**, working two stitches into each space of the open edge where possible, but only one if space does not allow for two (diagram 56). It is essential to keep the spacing of your stitches even, and you must judge for yourself where to make only one stitch into a loop instead of two. There is no need to lay a cord for this first row as you have the twisted bar of the open edge to work into.

Row 2. Lay a cord from **F** to **G** and continue to work corded Brussels until approximately one row before the position of the open vein. You must judge for yourself whether to slip only

16 Detail of Brussels Point de Gaze shown in photograph 14

once or perhaps twice into each space of the open edge when laying the cord across for each row.

To work the open vein

1. Whip into alternate loops for the length of the marked vein, then into one more loop past the vein. Now take the cord across the rest of the petal to the open edge. (Diagram 57)

2. Slip into the open edge loop, one or twice as the case may be, and increase the row by working one or possibly two stitches into the open edge. Work one stitch into every loop of the previous row until you reach the position of the vein. (Diagram 58)

3. Work a single Brussels stitch into the first loop, then a twisted buttonhole stitch into each alternate loop, working it into the loop that you did not whip into, in the same way as for the Gros Point sample (see p. 17). Continue to the end of the row. (Diagram 58)

4. Whip back into every large loop and into the first loop of the single Brussels. (Diagram 59)

5. Take the cord across to the open edge and slip once or twice, as required, into the appropriate space.

6. When you worked the Gros Point sample with veins, I mentioned that these were a useful way of increasing or decreasing in the middle of a row. Because of the curve of these rows, it may not be sufficient to increase at either end to maintain an even tension.

Instead of working *two* stitches into every loop of the open vein in the following row, work *three* stitches where you feel it is necessary. If you wish to decrease the number of stitches, then work only *one* stitch instead of two where required.

Make *one* stitch into each loop of the single Brussels worked in the previous row, and *two* single Brussels stitches into each large loop. (Diagram 60)

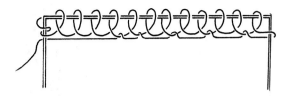

Diagram 57

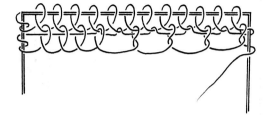

Diagram 58

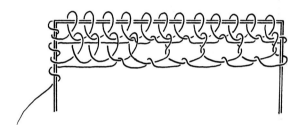

Diagram 59

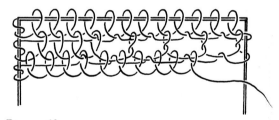

Diagram 60

7. Complete the petal, working a four hole diamond as you did in the Gros Point sample (see diagrams 4–8, pp. 14–16).

Petal 2

Work as for petal 1 but when you come to work the final row of corded Brussels stitch, you will

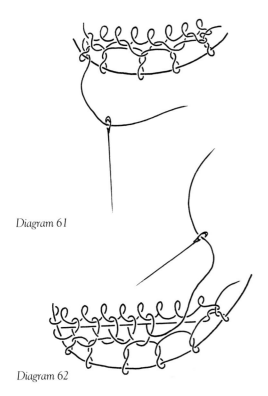

Diagram 61

Diagram 62

Petal 3

Work as for petal 1.

Areas 7 and 8

These areas form the folded edges of the petals (shown in diagram 53). Work in corded Brussels.

Petals 4, 5 and 6

These three petals are all worked using corded Brussels for the tips, and Point d'Espagne (twisted buttonhole stitch) for the remainder.

1. Score a line from the dotted line on each petal, back to the tips. This will again give you the position and angle of each row (see diagram 53).

2. Start with the centre section of Petal 4 and work as far as you can before reaching the right-hand section (diagram 63). Work this section and the left-hand one until you can work a row right across all three sections. Try to maintain a gentle curve.

3. Whip back into every other loop of the final row and leave.

4. Repeat this process for petals 5 and 6 (see diagram 53).

5. The remainder of each of the three petals is worked in twisted buttonhole stitch, but only into alternate loops of the corded Brussels. Work the first row by working into the stitch that you did not whip into. All subsequent rows are worked *without* a whipped return, in other words, one row from left to right, and the following row from right to left. Point de Gaze ground does *not* have a whipped return row.

need to attach it to the open edge. This can be done in two different ways.

Attaching the final row to an open edge

One method is to work the row as usual and then whip it to the open edge, taking the working thread round the vertical bar of the appropriate open edge stitch, enabling you to attach and fasten it to the cordonnet. (Diagram 61)

The second method is to lay the thread across from one side of the work to the other, and secure. Work the first stitch, then take the needle under the bottom of the open edge stitch and out into the hole. Make the next stitch, then take the needle under the bottom of the open edge as before and repeat to the end of the row. In this way you are attaching the final row to the open edge as you work it. Finally take the working thread round the vertical bar of the open edge stitch and fasten off. (Diagram 62)

Diagram 63

59

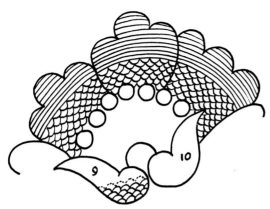

Diagram 64

To Work Small Wheels across the Centre

1. Attach the working thread at **C**, take it across to the first twisted ray and make a knot stitch or buttonhole stitch. Place your thumbnail on the stitch and pull the working thread tightly towards the ceiling. This will tighten the stitch and prevent it from slipping. (Diagram 66)

Proceed to the second ray and repeat for remaining rays. Anchor the thread at **D**.

2. The thread now has to return to **C** by twisting back over the thread just laid, to the first intersection. This will be the position for the first wheel. (Diagram 67)

(However, the ground for Alençon needlelace *does*, although Alençon techniques are not covered in this book.) Work each petal to the semi-circle of little rings. (Diagram 64)

It is extremely difficult to keep the tension even, but it will come with practice. You will find it easier to work each petal one at a time, but if you feel you can manage it, by all means work across the three petals in one go.

Petals 9 and 10

These petals are also worked in twisted buttonhole stitch, but the work will be covered by three-dimensional petals laid on top, so there is no need to be quite as particular about an even tension (diagram 64). It is therefore permissible to whip the return row if you find it easier.

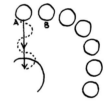

Diagram 65

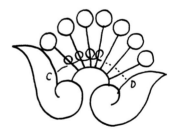

Diagram 66

To Work the Twisted Bars

Attach the working thread and whip along to the centre of the first ring to **A** in diagram 65, which is the position for the first bar. Take the working thread down to the semi-circle in the centre of the flower, making sure that the thread is taut. Secure and twist back up this thread three or four times to **A**; fasten the thread securely. Whip along to the second ring, position **B**, and repeat for remaining rays. (Diagram 65)

Diagram 67

3. Weave the thread round this intersection, passing over and under each of the four threads until the wheel is the required size, finishing at the position where you first started.

4. Take the thread under the wheel in the direction of the next intersection to be worked, and bring it up between the last two threads (this is to stop the wheel from slipping).

5. Twist the thread over the horizontal thread already laid to the position of the next wheel, but this time weave your wheel in the opposite direction. (One wheel should be woven clockwise, and the following wheel anticlockwise.) This again will prevent the wheel from becoming loose and slipping (diagram 68). These wheels can also be buttonholed over if desired, but as the upper rings will be buttonholed couronnes, the effect will be more pleasing with a contrast.

6. Work the small half-circle in the centre of the flower, below the woven wheels just worked, by folding one strand of Brok No. 24 in half. Work buttonhole stitches over these two threads, using Brok 100/3 for the stitching. When only one or two stitches are left to be worked, cut off the two Brok No. 24 threads on the diagonal, complete and secure.

The row of couronnes below the top three petals will be worked when the rest of the flower has been completed. This will prevent them from becoming grubby and will also make it far easier to work the cordonnette, as your working thread will not keep catching on these raised areas.

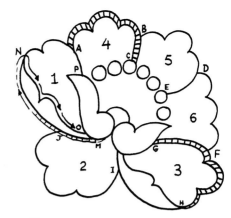

Diagram 69

To Work the Cordonnette

Petal 4

Start at **A** in diagram 69 with a length of Brok 24/3 doubled (making sure that you have allowed sufficient thread to work round petals 4, 5, 6 and 3). Work buttonhole stitches over these two threads, using Brok 100/3. It is not necessary for the stitches to be as close together for the Point de Gaze as for the Gros Point, because there are only two threads to cover, and the straight edge of the buttonhole stitch should be on the outside edge of the petal.

Continue round the top edge of this petal to **B**. At this point the petal comes in front of the next one (numbered 5, the central petal) and the edge of the buttonhole stitch must stay on the same side in order to create this effect. (Diagram 69)

Divide the cordonnette threads here, leaving one behind. Place a pin at **C** and take the second thread round the pin and back to **B** with the tail end extending, to join the one left behind (diagram 70). Work over the two threads to **C**. Take the needle under the cordonnette after working the final stitch; take out the pin and bring the needle through the loop left. This will prevent the stitches falling off the end when you gently pull the tail end of this thread to tighten the loop.

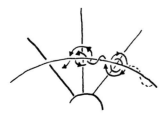

Diagram 68

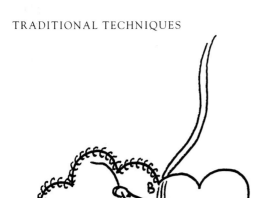

Diagram 70

fold the cordonnette thread back to form a loop, with the tail end extending to join the thread previously left behind. You are in fact repeating the same procedure performed in the previous two petals, but instead of using a pin to secure the thread, you are whipping it down into position first. Check the length of your working thread here, as this is an ideal opportunity to start a new thread if required.

Work over the two threads, back to **F**, and continue round to **H** until only one or two stitches need to be worked. Cut off the cordonnette threads closely and on the diagonal. Do be careful not to cut the working thread! Complete and fasten off the working thread.

The bottom edge of this petal turns over and also comes in front of petal 2. It is easier to work petal 2 now and to return to complete no. 3 later. (Diagram 69)

If the working thread is running short, secure and fasten off. If, however, the working thread is still of a reasonable length, take the needle back and forth and through the cordonnette, back to **B**, where you will have two threads ready to start working the next petal. (Diagram 70)

Petal 5

Work this second petal in the same manner to **D**, divide the threads and repeat to **E** as for petal 4. (Diagram 69)

Petal 6

You should have two threads at **D**. Work from **D** to **F** as for the previous petals. This completes the top three petals. (Diagram 69)

Petal 3

This petal comes in front of the previous one (no. 6) and so the edge of the buttonhole stitch has to be reversed to create this effect. (Diagram 69)

Divide the threads at **F**, leave one behind and take the needle under the cordonnette (this will prevent the final stitch from turning over). Take the second thread to **G**, whipping it down into position with the working thread. Secure with a couple of extra stitches, then

Petal 2

Start at **I** and work round to **J** until only one or two stitches need to be worked. Cut off the threads closely and on the diagonal and finish, *or* take the needle under the work, bringing it up at **M** (having left one thread behind) and bringing the other thread along to **M** by whipping it into place. Make a couple of firm stitches over the thread, and fold it back (as you have done several times previously) ready to start petal 1.

Return to petal 3

Start at **K** with a double thread, keeping the edge of the buttonhole stitch on the top (diagram 71), working on to **H** and round to **I** before finishing at **L** as before.

Petal 1

Commence at **M**, working the buttonhole stitch with the edge at the bottom of the petal (diagram 69), on to **N** and further to **O**, until only two stitches are left to be worked. Cut off

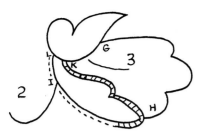

Diagram 71

Diagram 72

methods and applying them to the lace. For
Point de Gaze a third method is used, working
them directly onto the lace.

1. Start at **A** with two strands of Brok 24/3
doubled (four strands), and whip these down
round the ring until you are back at **A**. If you
start at either the centre-top or bottom of the
little rings, rather than where each joins the
other, they will be less bulky and far easier to
join when completed. (Diagrams 73 and 74)

2. Proceed to take these strands round in the
same direction a second time and make
buttonhole stitches close together over these
eight threads, but start approximately 2 mm.
(¹⁄₁₆ in.) past the beginning. (Diagram 75)

3. Cut the four padding threads on the
diagonal when only two or three stitches are
left to be worked before reaching the first stitch
worked. Join the ring by slipping into the first
loop, and secure by taking the needle back and
forth through the padding of the couronne
several times. Now cut the working thread (as
you did with the Gros Point couronnes).

the threads on the diagonal, work the last two
stitches, secure and finish.

Start at **N** by running in a new working thread
from the incomplete side of this petal to **N**.
Take the thread under the completed edge of
the petal at **N** (into the turned-back edge of
the petal already worked) and back again to
make certain that it is secure. Fold a length of
Brok 24/3 in half to form a loop, and take the
needle through this loop, *then back under the
completed cordonnette at **N***, and return. This
doubled thread should now appear to be
coming from behind the turned-over bottom
edge of this petal. Complete the edge to **P** and
finish as previously explained.

The shaded petals

As the shaded area of petals is to have another
layer placed on top, it is not necessary to work
a cordonnette right the way round. This would
make the area rather bulky when the other
petals are added. Only the top area indicated
need be worked. (Diagram 72)

To Work the Couronnes

In the Gros Point sample the couronnes were
worked on a ring stick or by using the 'trace'

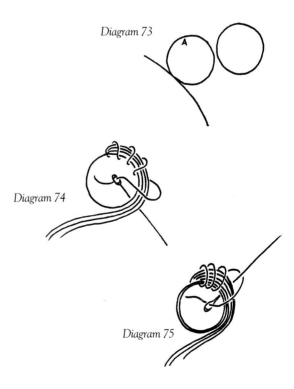

Diagram 73

Diagram 74

Diagram 75

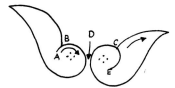

Diagram 76

4. Repeat the next ring in the same manner, but do not start where two rings touch each other. Each ring is worked completely separate – in other words, not overlapping each other.

The Separate Petal

This petal will have been worked in corded Brussels with four hole diamonds, as marked on the pattern.

1. Work cordonnette of the left-hand petal first. Start at **A** in diagram 76 with a doubled length of 24/3, and work Point d'Espagne (twisted buttonhole stitch) round to two or three stitches before **B**. Cut off the threads on the diagonal, and complete.

2. Work the right-hand petal the same way, starting at **C** and working round to **D**. Join the two petals together by working into the two stitches opposite on the first petal. Continue to **E** and complete.

Finally remove the work from its backing, clean, and stab stitch the extra petals into position on the main flower.

Fairly detailed instructions have been given for working the cordonnette, and this subject will not be covered again, as space does not allow for such detail in the following projects.

Pattern 5
Point de Gaze Flower Spray

The inspiration for this pattern came from the
beautiful lappet, which I have long admired,
from the Spriggs Collection (photograph 14).
The drooping leaf to the right of the spray has
been taken from the lappet and introduces
another method of shading, whilst the flower is
the same one already worked, but reduced in
size to accommodate a finer thread and
different fillings.

Materials Required

Brok cotton No. 36 for the cordonnet
Egyptian cotton No. 80 (or Copley Marshall
No. 80 if you have it) for the filling stitches

Note that all filling stitches are worked in
No. 80 thread.

Couching the Cordonnet

Use Brok No. 36 and couch down all veins in
the leaves and bottom three petals of the
flower. *Do not couch* rays from the couronnes in
the centre of the flower.

Pattern 5

Bud

The outside sepals of the bud are worked in corded Brussels stitch, incorporating open veins, whilst the actual bud is worked in twisted buttonhole stitch without a whipped return.

Leaves

Work the outside edges of the leaves with an open edge and whip back to strengthen, as for the petals in the previous flower. (Photograph 18)

Leaf 1

The curled edge is worked in corded Brussels, working the rows as indicated (diagram 77) and connecting to the open edge. The other half of the leaf is worked in twisted buttonhole stitch, working the stitches the same distance apart as for the open edge. Work the stitches from left to right and whip back into every loop from right to left (or the opposite way round if you are left handed). All buttonhole rows are worked in the same direction. (Photograph 18)

Diagram 78

Diagram 79

Leaves 2 and 3

Both are worked with an open edge and filled with corded Brussels, but the area within the dotted line and close to the central vein is worked in twisted buttonhole stitch with a whipped return, which creates the shaded effect. (Diagram 77)

Shaded Area

Leaf 3

Refer to diagram 77. Work corded Brussels, starting at the bottom of the leaf. (See also photograph 18.)

To start the shaded area

1. Whip into alternate loops for the length to be shaded, plus one more loop. Take the cord across to the open edge, as you did for the open vein in the previous flower. (Diagram 78)

2. Work a single Brussels stitch into every loop of the previous row until you reach the second whipped loop. Miss this loop and work a *twisted* buttonhole stitch into the next loop (diagram 79) and every alternate loop (the one that you did not whip into) to the end of the row.

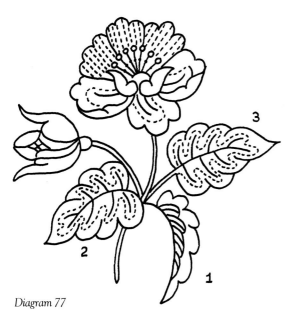

Diagram 77

Flower spray designed and worked by the author. (Pattern 5)

17 Brussels bobbin and needlelace plastron. The central
flower motif has been used by Marjory Crump for her
tea-cosy design (see pattern section, p. 172).

18 Detail of flower spray

3. Whip back into every large loop plus one small loop, then take the cord across to the open edge. (Diagram 80)

4. Work a single Brussels stitch into every loop until you reach the first whipped loop. *Miss this first whipped loop* and work a *twisted* buttonhole stitch into the *second* whipped loop. Continue to work a twisted buttonhole stitch into every loop to the end. (Diagram 81)

You can now see that you are gradually extending the shaded area. The shading can of course be increased more rapidly, by whipping into more than just one extra loop of each row. It really depends on the shape of the area required, and you can extend by as many loops as you wish.

Reverse the process by making *two* stitches into a large loop to reduce the length of the shaded

Diagram 80

Diagram 81

area. Work all three leaves and the bottom three petals using this technique. (Diagram 77)

Top Three Petals

These are worked in twisted buttonhole stitch (without a whipped return), working the rows as indicated. (Diagram 77)

Raised Spots

Work these spots at random on the top three petals, by working three buttonhole stitches over the top of the completed net.

1. Run the needle under the buttonhole stitches from right to left, leaving a reasonable tail of thread extending (diagram 82). Approximately 6 cm. (2½ in.) will be sufficient. Now work three buttonhole stitches from left to right, over this thread and the net ground beneath. (Diagram 83)

2. Take the working thread right round the group of stitches and work a buttonhole stitch, making sure that the working thread is to the right of the needle. Enclose this group of stitches (diagram 83), but do not pull the thread too tightly until you have taken the needle from right to left under the vertical bars

19 Detail of Point de Gaze lappet (see photograph 14)

of the three stitches to secure the working thread. Now pull the thread gently and cut off. Take great care not to cut the ground beneath! Finally cut the tail end that was left extending to the right. I have not yet found an antique sample where the majority of these spots have not worked loose, so it is advisable not to cut the threads too close.

Area under the Raised Petals

This is also worked in twisted buttonhole stitch just as you did for the previous flower. You could whip the return row if you find it easier, but this is an ideal place to get in some practice without whipping, as it will not be visible in the finished piece. The more you practise, the better you will become, and it will pay off in the end!

Central Rays with Rosebud Knots

Work as for the previous flower, but this time Rosebud knots are worked instead of woven wheels.

1. Lay each ray and twist back.

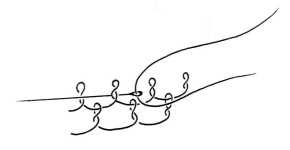

Diagram 82

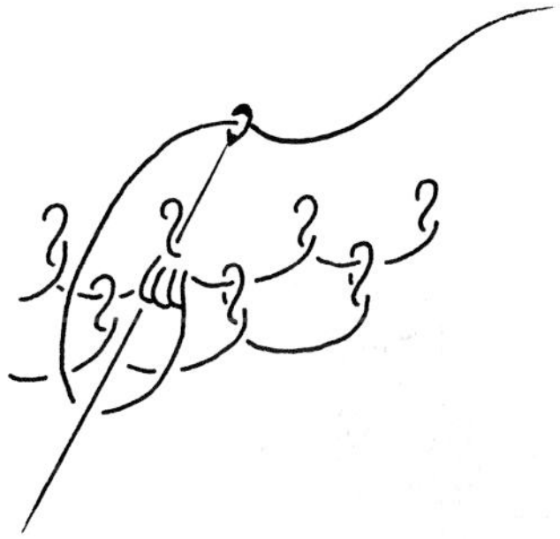

Diagram 83

71

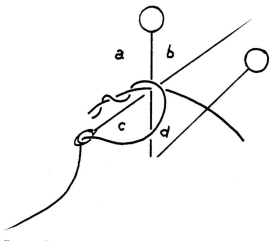

Diagram 84

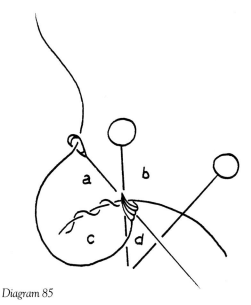

Diagram 85

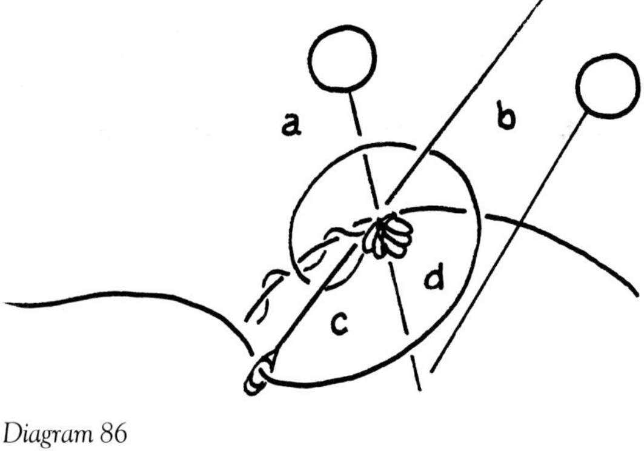

2. Take the horizontal thread across from one side to the other, knotting at each intersection.

3. Check that your working thread is long enough to return, making little Rosebud knots along the way. If you are in any doubt, then run in a new length of thread at this stage. Whip along the horizontal thread (two or three times) to the intersection, and take the working thread under the crossing by putting the needle in at **c** and bringing it out at **b**. (Diagram 84)

4. Turn the work a little and make three buttonhole stitches over the intersection, by putting the needle in at **a** and bringing it out at **d**. (Diagram 85)

5. Turn the work a little once again, and make two buttonhole stitches diagonally over the first three stitches, by taking the needle in at **b** and out at **c**.

6. Make a buttonhole stitch right round the five stitches already worked, by taking the needle over the working thread and in at **c**. Take it under the intersection, over the working thread and out at **b** (diagram 86). Gently ease the thread, putting your thumbnail over the loop to make sure it goes right round and underneath the edges of the stitches. Pull the working thread tightly to enclose these stitches, making a little Rosebud.

Twist across to the next intersection and repeat for the remaining rays.

The little knot in the centre of the flower bud is worked in the same way.

Diagram 86

20 Detail of a Point de Gaze flounce from the Devonshire Collection at Chatsworth House

Extra Petals

These are worked in corded Brussels with four hole diamonds.

The Cordonnette

Work the whole spray using four strands of No. 80 thread doubled. You should now be able to work the cordonnette without any further instruction, but remember that the stem comes from behind the flower and should be worked first. Next work the leaves and bud, remembering to work the veins in the leaves.

The flower is the same as for pattern 4, but remember to work the veins in the bottom three petals.

The Couronnes

These are left until last and are worked as for pattern 4, but using four strands of working thread doubled (eight in all) instead of only one doubled. By the time you come to work the buttonhole stitches (second time round) you will actually be working over sixteen threads. (Photograph 21)

The Separate Petals

The cordonnette for these is worked with a *twisted* buttonhole stitch, which gives a rather nice effect. Finally remove from the backing material and stab stitch to the main flower.

21 Detail of flower spray showing couronnes in the process of being worked

Scrolls

Pattern 6
Scroll with Daisy Wheels and Rosebud Wheels

Materials Required

Brok cotton No. 24 for cordonnet
Brok cotton No. 100/3 for filling stitches
Egyptian cotton Nos 80 and 120 for wheels

1. Areas **A** in diagram 87 are both worked in corded Brussels, working the rows along the longer length.

2. The main scroll is worked in corded Brussels, with a short length of open vein in the centre of the curve (marked with a continuous line) and a four hole diamond, as indicated in diagram 87.

Scrolls with a variety of wheels are a prominent feature of Point de Gaze (see photograph 20), but often a student will work little short straight rows, instead of following the line of the curve, which really does not enhance the work at all. You have learnt how to join a new thread in the middle of a long row when

working the Hollie Point sample. To ensure that you do not pull the stretched cord too tightly, you must slip into the occasional loop along the length of the curve, as you did for the Hollie Point. Intervals of approximately 3–4 cm. (1–1¼ in.) would be about the correct distance. It is extremely difficult to work the length of your rows from one end of the scroll to the other. Look at diagram 87: you will need to be on the dotted line from **b–b** to work the small circular area at one end.

Take your needle or scissors and score the pattern lightly from **b** to **b** and back along the scroll, making the first long line end at **c** in diagram 87. You can now see that it will be quite simple to work the small area remaining at this end. Continue to score lines back for the entire curve and you will notice that the right-hand side of the scroll begins to widen, but carry on until the area is filled, reducing the length of each row. You will see from diagram 87 that there are two short rows marked **d–d** and **e–e**. This will give you the length and angle of the first row to be worked. It is only a rough guideline, but will help you to visualise how the scroll will progress.

1. Work the scroll, starting the first row from **e–e** and the second row from **d–d**.

2. The third row (or it may possibly be your fourth, depending on your tension) is the first long row, going from one end of the scroll to the other. Take the cord across, slipping into the occasional loop at intervals of approximately 3–4 cm. (1–1¼ in.). Keep it fairly slack, and buttonhole stitch back. Repeat this process where required in subsequent rows; however, do not slip the cord into the same place for each row – slip it a little further along each time. If you whip it in the same place it will become more noticeable and resemble the decreasing process used when knitting a raglan sleeve. (This could, on the other hand, be quite useful when working a piece of clothing for stumpwork, in order to accentuate a crease in the crook of an arm or leg.)

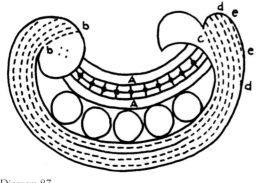

Diagram 87

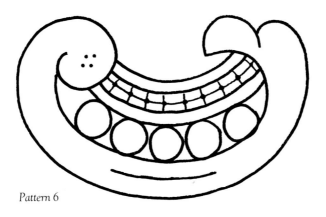

Pattern 6

22 Scroll designed and worked by the author (pattern 6)

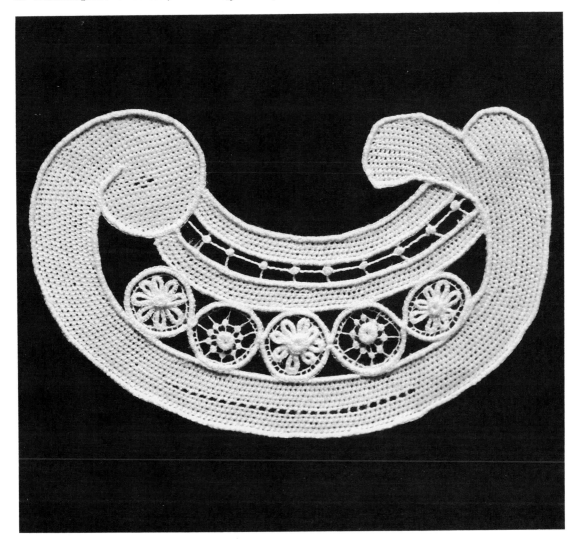

3. As the work progresses, make an open vein where indicated. If you find your stitches are becoming too densely packed in the centre of the curve, this is an ideal opportunity to lose one or two by working only one stitch instead of two into the occasional space when completing the vein.

4. Continue until you reach row **b** (diagram 87). From here work the rows across from one side to the other, making a four hole diamond as indicated.

5. Complete the other end of the scroll, following the curve as indicated. (Diagram 88)

Rosebud Knots

Work these where indicated on the pattern, working the short rows first, then the long row, just as you did for the flower in pattern 5.

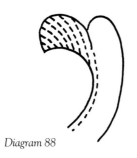

Diagram 88

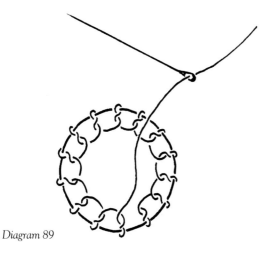

Diagram 89

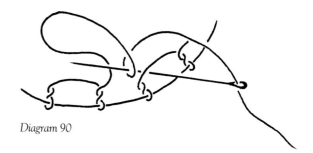

Diagram 90

Wheels with Rosebud Knots

A much finer thread is required for these wheels, but try a larger sample first, using Brok 100/3 for the working thread instead of the 120 Egyptian cotton. Work twisted buttonhole stitch evenly spaced round the ring. (Diagram 89)

To Join the Ring

1. Place your needle into the *first* loop worked, then turn it towards the *last* stitch worked and make another twisted buttonhole stitch. Think of it as working a twisted buttonhole stitch sideways on. The thread is now in the correct position to whip back, having joined the ring (diagram 90). Whip back *only halfway* round the ring.

2. You will need to lay four rays across the wheel. Take the working thread from the top to the bottom of the wheel, into the whipped loop, and whip back (diagram 91). Make sure that the thread is taut. If these rays are not taut it will be extremely difficult to weave round them for the next stage of the work.

3. Whip round the ring to the position of the next ray and repeat. (Diagram 92)

4. Repeat until all four rays have been laid and check that you have sufficient working thread to complete the remainder of the ring and a couronne. If in doubt renew your thread before twisting back. Whip back *only to the centre of*

23 Detail of an antique Point de Gaze collar, showing the use of Daisy wheels and Rosebud wheels

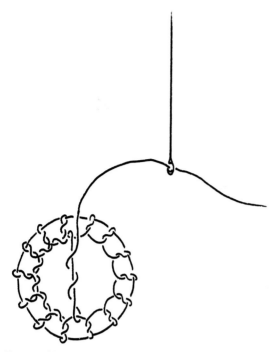

Diagram 91

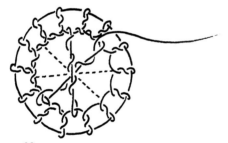

Diagram 92

down round the central hub, then remove the pin. It is important to start at the single unwhipped ray, because if you start here you will obviously finish here, and it is this single ray that you will whip along to the position required for the next stage of the work.

Take the threads round a second time and complete the couronne as you did for the previous flower. Join the couronne and cut off the surplus threads, but *do not cut* the working thread.

7. You will now be able to whip halfway down the single ray and knot the working thread to this ray. Pass on to the next ray and repeat to complete the circle.

8. Work round a second time, whipping to the thread already laid and making Rosebud knots at each intersection. (Diagram 93)

9. Finally whip down the remainder of the single ray, over the loop into the few open-edge stitches left unwhipped, and over the twisted vertical bar of the nearest open-edge stitch. Secure to the cordonnet (diagram 93). *N.B.* Use No. 120 thread for the actual sample, with No. 80 to pad the couronne.

the wheel for the fourth ray, and knot. All rays will be twisted *except* half of the final ray.

5. Place a pin in the centre of the wheel and *weave* the working thread under and over round the pin three or four times, finishing the weaving at the single untwisted ray. This will give you a foundation on which to work the central couronne, which needs to have extra threads whipped down.

6. Leave the pin in position (you will need this to make a hole in the centre), take two lengths of Brok No. 24 folded in half, and whip them

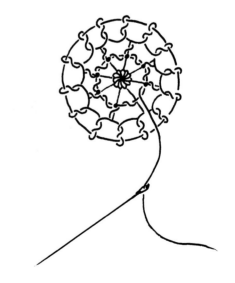

Diagram 93

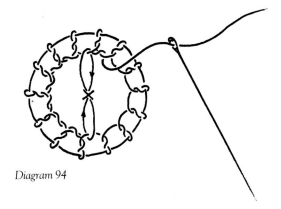

Diagram 94

large sample use 100/3). Take the needle under the crossed trace threads in the centre, with a tail end extending parallel with the thread of the first petal, and knot (diagram 96). Take the working thread through the loop of the four folded threads and proceed to work a *twisted* buttonhole stitch over these threads along with the laid thread (and tail end of the new working thread), down one side of the petal to the base. Work into the open edge at the base (this will prevent the petals from turning

Daisy Wheels

Tips before you start

If you have had difficulty making the knot secure in the centre of your wheel, resulting in an off-centre couronne, try scoring the rays with your needle, then make two tiny 'trace' stitches (as you did for the Gros Point sample) to form a cross in the centre. When laying the threads from one side of the wheel to the other, take the working thread under these stitches. This should ensure that they cross in the centre.

1. Work as for the previous wheel, with an open edge, but instead of whipping back along each ray, take the needle from the bottom of the wheel back up to the top, passing under the crossed trace stitches in the centre, to form a loop. (Diagram 94)

2. Whip round to the position of the next petal and repeat. Continue in this fashion twice more, making eight petals in total. (Diagram 95)

3. When the last petal has been laid, whip round the few remaining edge stitches back to the beginning. Take the working thread over the vertical bar of the edge stitch and secure to the cordonnet.

4. Take four lengths of 120 thread doubled (if you are trying a larger sample first, use one length of Brok No. 24 doubled). Thread the needle with a long length of 120 thread (for a

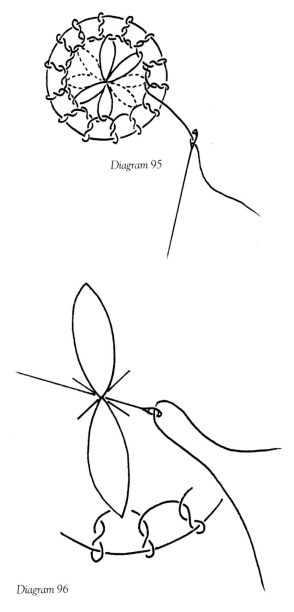

Diagram 95

Diagram 96

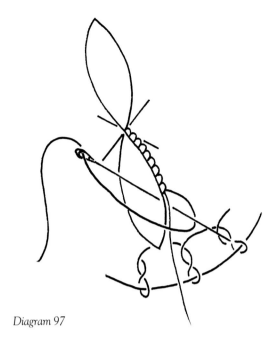

Diagram 97

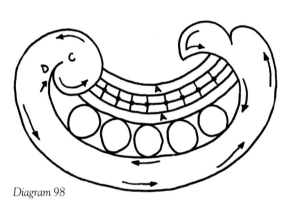

Diagram 98

over), then back up the other side to the centre of the daisy. (Diagram 97)

5. Take the needle under the central hub to secure the loose threads. Repeat this action a second time, taking the needle over the bundle

of loose threads to secure them, before working the next petal. Repeat for all eight petals. *Do not cut off these threads* as they will now be used to make the couronne.

The Central Couronne

Check that your working thread is long enough to complete the couronne. If in any doubt, now is the time to renew it. Alternatively, use one in the bundle of loose threads, if it happens to be long enough.

The loose threads should now be in the centre of the daisy. Place a pin in the centre of the flower and whip these threads down round the pin. Finally buttonhole stitch round and complete, as you will have done many times by now.

The Cordonnette

Take four lengths of 80 thread folded in half, and buttonhole stitch over these, using the 80 thread for stitching also.

1. Refer to diagram 98. Work areas **A** first, as these come from behind the scroll.

2. Start the scroll at **C**, working round to **D**, and finish cutting the threads on the diagonal.

3. Finally work the cordonnette round the wheels. They could be worked separately as for the couronnes in the centre of the flower in pattern 5, or worked first along one side and then the other. Use eight strands doubled instead of four if you are going to follow this second method, because you will only be working round once. If you work them individually like a couronne, you will go round twice and will need only four doubled.

Pattern 7
Scroll Incorporating Rosebud Knots

Materials Required

Brok cotton No. 36 for cordonnet
Egyptian cotton No. 80

Tips before you start

Score the pattern back from the circular areas at either end, as you did for the previous scroll, to give the approximate angle and position of the first row. If you found it difficult to control the positioning of your rows, try drawing the lines on the pattern before covering with the sticky-backed plastic or architect's linen. I find that a dark-blue covering is far less tiring on the eyes, and makes the stitches easier to see against the dark background.

1. Work both areas marked **A** in corded Brussels. (Diagram 99)

2. Work area **B** in corded Brussels with a small diamond in the circular area at the end, just as you did for the scroll in pattern 6.

3. Area **C** is worked in corded Brussels, starting the first row **d–d**, as indicated in diagram 99. Complete as for the previous scroll (photograph 25). You could work a small open vein where a continuous line is shown in diagram 99.

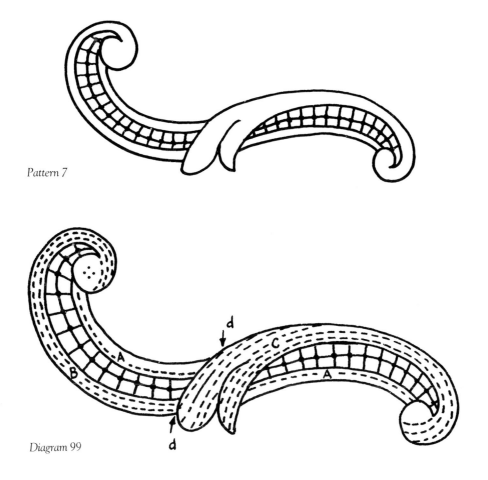

Pattern 7

Diagram 99

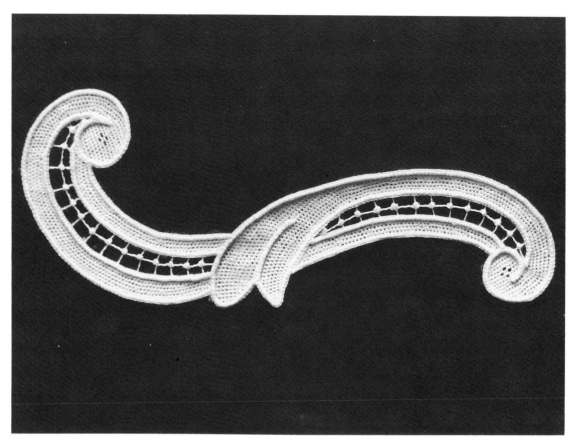

24 Scroll designed and worked by the author (pattern 7)

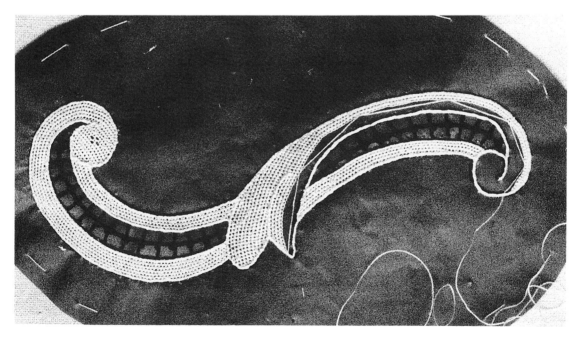

25 Partly worked scroll (pattern 7)

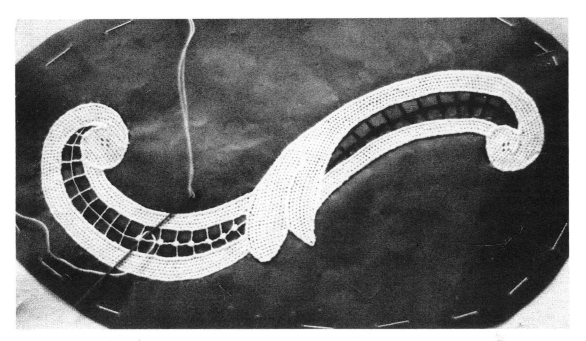

26 The partly worked scroll (pattern 7), incorporating
Rosebud knots

4. Work Rosebud knots as indicated.
(Photograph 26)

The Cordonnette

Use four strands of No. 80 thread doubled
(eight strands). Work areas **A** first, as these
come from behind the main scroll (see
photograph 24).

Pattern 8
Scroll with Scalloped Edge and Couronnes

Pattern 8

Materials Required

Brok No. 36 for the cordonnet
Egyptian cotton No. 80

Areas A

Refer to diagram 100. Work in corded Brussels.

Area B

Work in corded Brussels.

Score the pattern back from the scroll end
with a small diamond (diagram 100).
Commence at **a–a** and complete as indicated.
(Photograph 27)

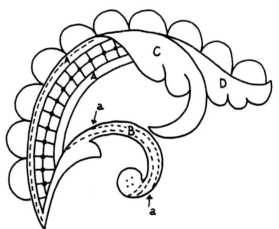

Diagram 100

27 Detail of partly worked scroll (pattern 8)

Area C

Study the area first to decide which line of the
curve to follow. Diagram 101 shows one
direction, which to my mind does nothing at
all to enhance the work. Diagram 102 shows
another. Both follow a natural curve but
diagram 102 gives a better effect, lending
greater charm to the work.

28 The completed scroll (pattern 8) designed and
worked by the author

Diagram 101

Diagram 102

Always start by marking in the line of a vein, then follow the natural curve from there. In this way, you should achieve the best effect. Score the pattern back from the vein marked **b–b** in diagram 103, continuing on to the vein marked **c–c** and further to **d–d**. Start the first row at **d–d**, working open veins where indicated.

Area D

Work area **D** (diagram 100), following the curve and working veins as indicated. (Photograph 29)

Scalloped Edge

1. Work one row of open edge round the first scallop. Either end will do.

2. Whip back into every loop.

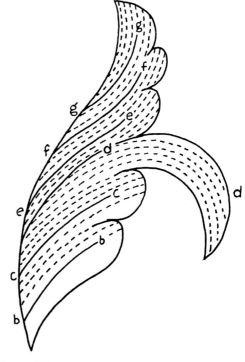

Diagram 103

88

1. Work the short twisted bars.

2. Take the working thread from one end to the other, knotting at each intersection.

3. Insert a pin at the intersection and make a woven wheel by taking the working thread over and under the horizontal and vertical threads. Three or four times should be sufficient. (Diagram 104)

4. Remove the pin and work buttonhole stitches over the woven wheel. Start at **A** so that you finish at **A** (diagram 105). Join the ring and whip to the next intersection. Repeat for all rings.

The Cordonnette

Use four strands doubled (making eight) of the same thread used for the filling stitches.

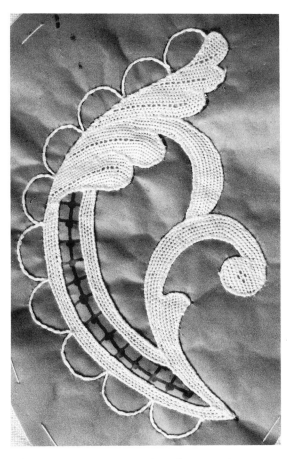

29 Detail of the partly worked scroll (pattern 8), illustrating the use of veins

3. Work single Brussels into every space, sometimes working two stitches into a space, sometimes only one. The radius of this row is slightly smaller than that of the previous one, so it is for you to use your own judgement. (Photograph 31)

4. Whip back into every loop and work a second row of single Brussels, missing the occasional loop as required.

5. Whip back into every loop and secure the working thread. Repeat for the remaining scallops.

Buttonholed Rings (Couronnes)

The preparation for these rings is the same as for the Rosebud wheels worked for pattern 7.

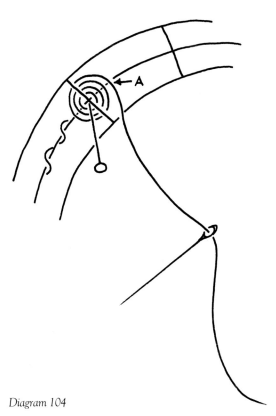

Diagram 104

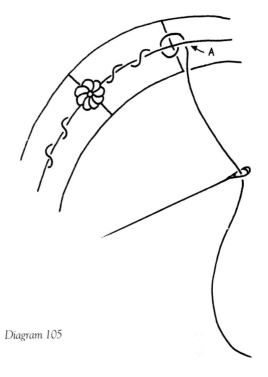

Diagram 105

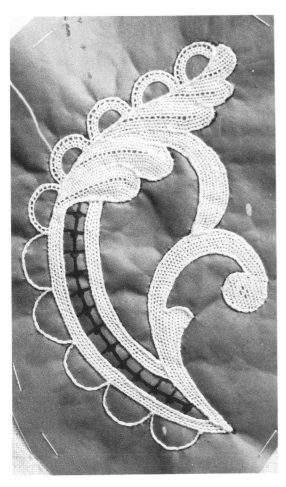

31 Detail of the scalloped edge

Study the sample first, and remember to divide the threads when necessary, making sure that the leaf section is worked so that it appears to come over the top of the scroll. You should already know how to do this. (Remember how you worked the first Point de Gaze flower.)

30 Point de Gaze flounce from the Devonshire Collection, Chatsworth House, Derbyshire

Pattern 9
Combination Scroll with Grid Filling

Diagram 106

Materials Required

Brok No. 36 for cordonnet
Egyptian cotton Nos 80 and 120

The Cordonnet

Use Brok No. 36 and couch down only lines shown on diagram 106. *Do not* couch lines for grid-filling area **A**, tiny couronnes (areas **B**), or dotted line on lower petal of the flower. This pattern is based on pattern 8, and does not therefore require detailed instructions. Work as before.

Double-ended Scroll

One of the rings at the end of the scroll is worked first (diagram 107). Work corded Brussels from **a** to **b** and continue until the ring is completed, incorporating a small diamond.

32 Completed scroll (pattern 9) designed and worked by the author

Pattern 9

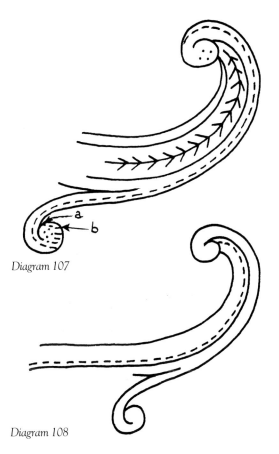

Diagram 107

Diagram 108

Follow the outside edge of the scroll and complete as for patterns 6 and 7.

The Fern Leaf

Work the net background in twisted buttonhole stitch, using the 120 thread. There are two ways to do this. I chose to work mine as for the previous scrolls, along the curve of the scroll. (Diagram 108)

Obviously the radius of the curve increases at some points and decreases at others, making it necessary when working the background to miss an occasional stitch. Try to do this when approaching the central stem. Any slight unevenness in the tension will not be quite so obvious when the final cordonnette has been worked. (Photographs 32 and 33)

Close examination of an antique sample revealed that the rows were worked on the diagonal and parallel with the leaves. One side was worked first, then the other. The second side was started from the opposite end, but this

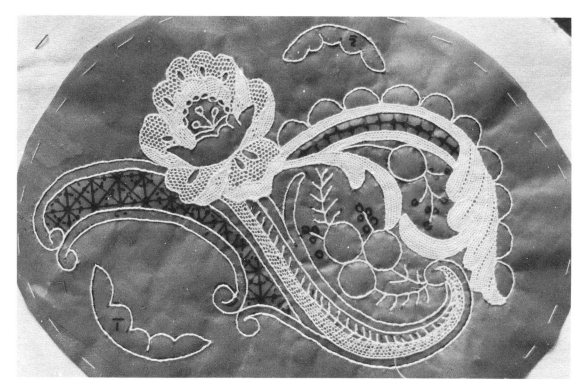

33 Scroll showing detail of fern leaf being worked (pattern 9)

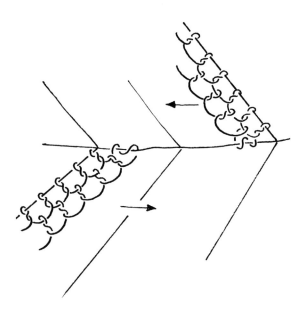

Diagram 109

is not visible to the naked eye (diagram 109). On close examination under a powerful magnifying glass, it can be seen that the background net of a good many antique samples is quite irregular. The thread used was so very much finer than that available today, and this is why the uneven tension is not nearly as obvious as in contemporary samples.

Cordonnette for the Fern Leaves

1. Take two strands of 80 thread doubled, and whip these down into position over the top of the net, using the 120 thread for the stitching and attaching it to the previously couched cordonnet.

2. Work the cordonnette using No. 120 thread and working Point d'Espagne (twisted buttonhole stitch). Try to imagine a zip fastener for this stage of the work. Both sides of the stem and leaves have to be worked, so it is necessary to space the stitches far enough apart to enable those stitches worked up the second side of each stem and leaf to fit between those worked on the first side. (Diagram 110)

Start at the base of the stem and proceed to work along the side of the first leaf, round the top, and along the other side, making each stitch between those on the first side, just like a zip fastener. (Diagram 110)

Areas B: Tiny Couronnes

These tiny couronnes are worked on top of the previously worked net, which is worked in the No. 120 thread. I found it took several attempts to secure the end of the working thread, as each time I tried to pull it tightly to do so, I managed to pull it out completely. The

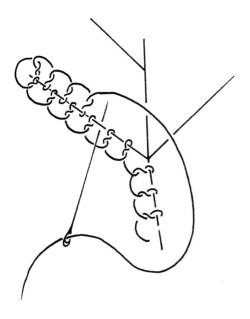

Diagram 110

Combination scroll designed and worked by the author.
(Pattern 9)

following method, using a fourth thread, worked every time.

1. Cut three lengths of No. 80 thread and a fourth, which will be roughly twice the length of the other three. Thread the needle with the longest length of thread and fold the other three in half to form a loop.

2. Fold the length of thread in the needle, and include it with the other three. Make a buttonhole stitch with the other end, over the doubled lengths of thread. (Diagram 111)

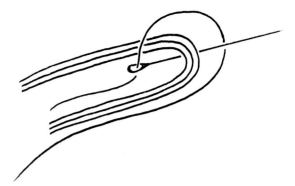

Diagram 111

3. Place a pin in the net background where you wish to make a couronne, as you did for the buttonholed rings down the centre of the previous scroll. Whip these seven threads down round the pin. Placing a pin in the work will enable you to pull the threads into a neat

ring without distorting the net background that you have already worked so carefully.

4. Make a tiny couronne by buttonhole stitching over these threads, just as you have done before, but leave the pin in the work as

34 Detail showing background net and tiny couronnes

Diagram 112

long as you can to avoid pulling on the net background.

5. When only two or three stitches are left to be worked, cut the laid threads on the diagonal and complete the ring.

The Flower

Work in 80 thread.

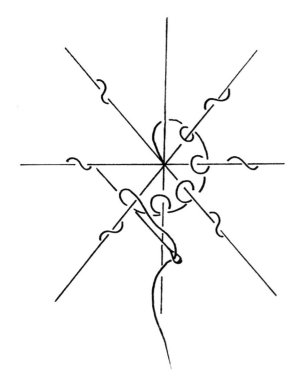

Diagram 113

Bottom petal

1. Take one strand of 80 thread, pass it under the cordonnet at **a** in diagram 112 to join, then continue to couch it down *doubled*, over the dotted line and across to the other side of the petal. Take one end under the cordonnet. *Do not cut off these ends*, but use each one in turn to work the filling stitches.

2. Work corded Brussels and Point d'Espagne as indicated on diagram 112.

Wheels

This sample has four different wheels. The Daisy wheel and Rosebud knot wheel you are already familiar with. All wheels are worked in 120 thread and 80 thread, the No. 120 for a working thread and the No. 80 for padding the couronnes.

Wheel 3: Spider web wheel

1. Work one round of open edge, join and whip back.

2. Work a second round of open edge into the loops of the first round. Join the ring and whip back only halfway round the ring.

3. Lay four rays, whipping back along three of them, but only to the centre of the fourth ray, and knot.

4. Work a woven wheel in the centre by taking the needle under two threads and back over one (diagram 113). Think of it as making a back-stitch. Repeat until the raised wheel is the required size, finishing the weaving opposite the untwisted ray. (Diagram 114)

5. Take the needle under the wheel, bringing it up inside the final round that was worked, and next to the untwisted ray (diagram 114). This will prevent the wheel from becoming slack.

6. Finally twist down this single ray and whip

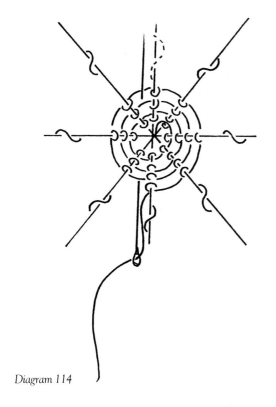

Diagram 114

7. You have now made a couronne in the centre and joined it, finishing at the unwhipped ray. (Check the length of your working thread. If it is too short to make six more couronnes, fasten off as for the couronnes worked in the first flower. Run in a new thread from the outer edge of the wheel by whipping up the single ray to commence the first couronne.)

Take the working thread down the single ray to the position for the first outer couronne and knot. Pass on to the next ray and knot. Repeat for all rays.

8. Take the thread round a second time, place a pin at the intersection and *weave* round the pin two or three times, forming a foundation for the couronne, then whip down four strands of No. 80 thread for the couronne.

9. Work round a second time, buttonhole stitching to make a couronne. Complete in the usual manner, then whip on to the next intersection and repeat for each couronne.

10. Whip down the final ray, along the vertical bar of the edge stitch and fasten.

into the few remaining loops of the second round of open edge. Take the working thread round the vertical bars of the twisted edge, to the outside of the ring, and secure.

Wheel 4: Couronne flower

This wheel requires only six rays, using 120 thread for the working thread and 80 for the padding for couronnes.

Refer to pattern 6, pp. 78–80, and work as for the wheel with Rosebud knots from stage 1 to stage 6, bearing in mind that you will have only six rays instead of eight, and will be working with a finer thread. Use four strands of 80 thread doubled for the central couronne and outer ring of couronnes.

The remainder of the wheel is worked as for the Rosebud knot wheel, but incorporating tiny couronnes instead of Rosebud knots.

Grid Filling 1

Try a sample first, using No. 80 thread. Couch down a square 4 cm. × 4 cm. (1¾ in. approx.).

1. Lay vertical threads 1 cm. (⅜ in.) apart from **a**–**b** in diagram 115, then whip back from **b**–**a**. These threads must be kept taut.

2. Lay horizontal threads 1 cm. apart from **c**–**d**, then whip back from **d**–**c**. (Diagram 116)

3. Lay diagonal threads from **e**–**f** and whip back. (Diagram 117)

4. Make sure that your thread is long enough to work the complete diagonal. If you find it is running short, the woven wheel at each intersection is an ideal place to run in a new

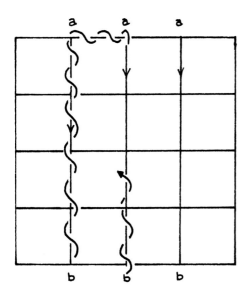

Diagram 115

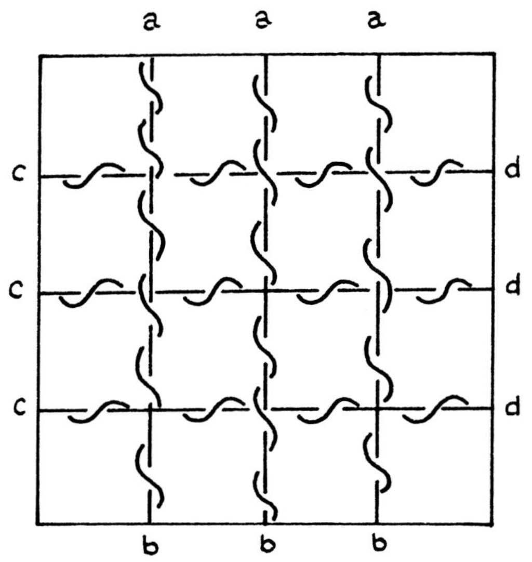

Diagram 116

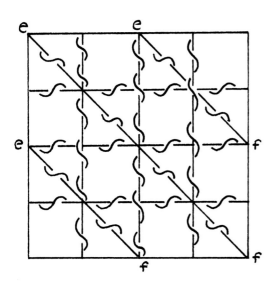

Diagram 117

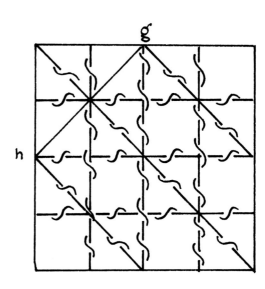

Diagram 118

thread. Lay a diagonal thread from **g–h**. (Diagram 118)

The couronnes

5. Whip back to the first intersection, place a pin in the centre and weave round the pin, starting at the remaining untwisted ray. Three

or four times should be sufficient, but this will vary according to the gauge of thread and size that you wish the couronne to be.

6. Leave the pin in position as long as you are able, and buttonhole stitch over this woven wheel, beginning again at the *untwisted ray*. The reason for starting at this position is that you will obviously also finish here. Join the couronne by slipping between the first two worked stitches, then whip approximately halfway along the untwisted ray and make a knot stitch. (Diagram 119)

7. Take the thread onto the next ray and knot. Continue round all eight rays and knot, returning to **i**. (Diagram 120)

8. Take the working thread round once more, whipping to the thread already laid, and work a Rosebud knot at each intersection. This will bring you back to the place where you started.

9. Work round once more, using the twisted horizontal threads between each Rosebud knot as a foundation cord, and work Point d'Espagne (twisted buttonhole stitch) between the knots. Two stitches between each knot should be sufficient, but again this will vary depending on the gauge of thread and the diameter of the ring of knots. Join the ring by slipping into the first loop. (Diagram 121)

10. Whip up the remainder of the untwisted diagonal ray to the next intersection. Make a woven wheel, then buttonhole stitch over this

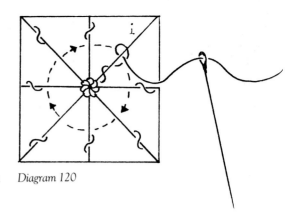

Diagram 120

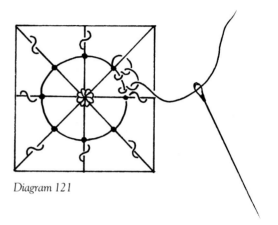

Diagram 121

to form a couronne. This intersection has a central couronne only. (Diagram 122)

11. Whip on to the next intersection and make a central couronne, then Rosebud knots as before (stages 5–9).

12. Repeat stage 10. Work alternate Rosebud knot wheels, with central couronnes only, to fill the entire space. (Photograph 35)

To complete the flower

Work the three central stems and couronnes as for the fern leaves and couronnes.

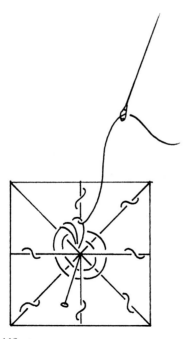

Diagram 119

35 Detail of Point de Gaze collar, showing grid filling 1 (bottom right) and grid filling 2 (centre right)

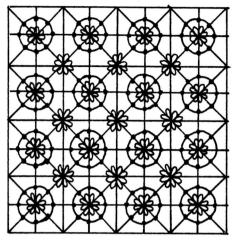

Diagram 122

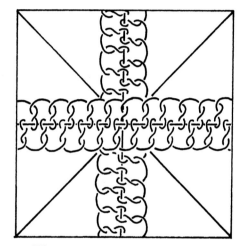

Diagram 123

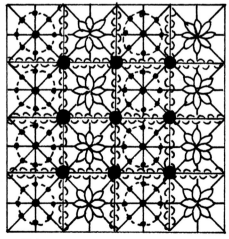

Diagram 124

The cordonnette

This is worked using four strands of No. 120 thread doubled, and No. 120 thread for the stitching also.

The small openings in the petals can be left without any filling at all, or make Rosebud knots using No. 120 thread.

Grid Filling 2

This is an alternative filling, which could be used for some of the patterns at the back of the book. The principle is the same, but Daisy wheels are worked, alternating with Rosebud knot wheels (see photograph 35). Repeat stages 1 and 2 (see diagrams 115 and 116, p. 99) of the previous grid filling.

3. Work Point d'Espagne down one side only of each vertical thread, spacing them far enough apart to accommodate two stitches into each loop. If you find this a little difficult, try putting in the odd 'trace' stitch to hold the vertical thread in position.

4. Turn the lace and work Point d'Espagne down the other side of each vertical bar, working the stitches between those of the first side. Imagine the zip fastener again.

5. Repeat for the horizontal bars. (Diagram 123)

6. Lay one set of diagonal threads as for the previous filling, and whip back.

7. Lay the second set of diagonal threads and work across the diagonal (as you did for the previous grid filling), making Daisy wheels and Rosebud wheels into alternate squares, and couronnes into the corner of each square (diagram 124, and see photograph 35). You will of course need to scale down these grid fillings to the correct size for your chosen pattern.

You have now worked samples of several major types of classic needlelace. Examples of others can be found in the following pages 103–11.

Classic Needlelace:
Some Antique Samples

36 Irish Youghal handkerchief

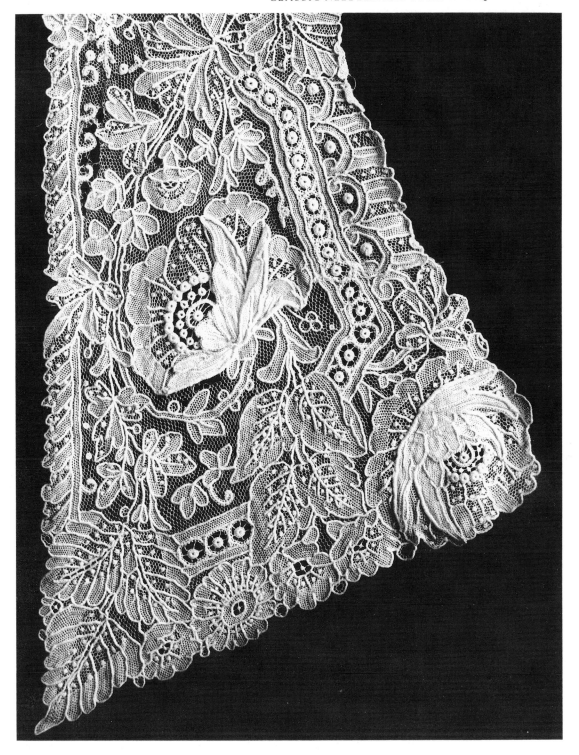

37 Brussels Point de Gaze

38 Point de Gaze collar from the Anne Aldridge
Collection

39 Point d'Argentan

40 Pair of eighteenth-century Alençon lappets

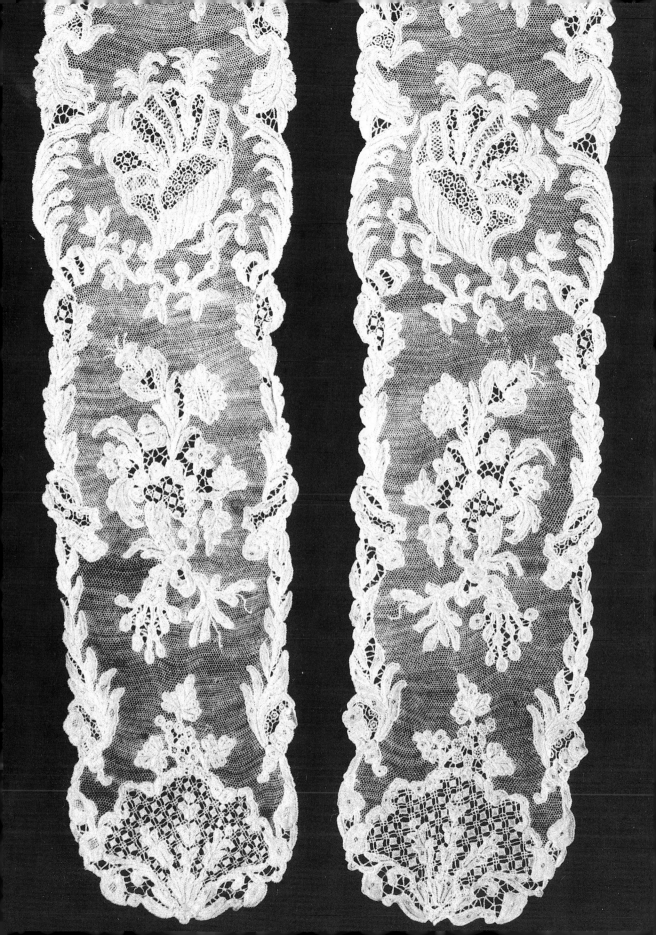

41 Detail of Alençon lappet (see photograph 40)

42 Detail of Alençon lappet (see photograph 40)

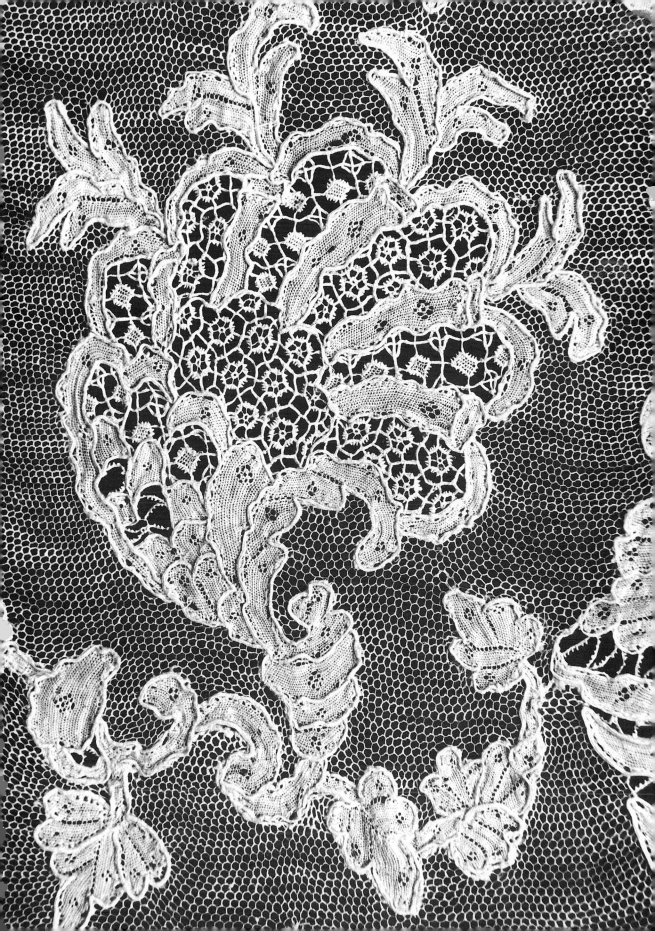

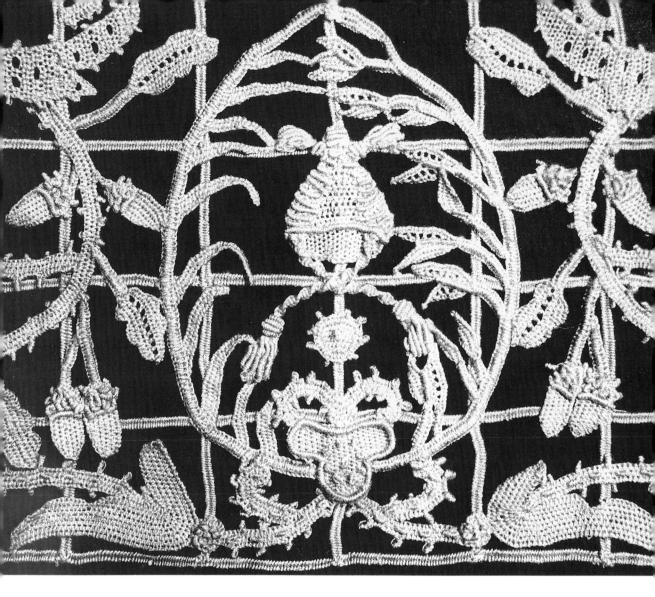

43 Aemelia Ars nineteenth-century reproduction from the Spriggs Collection

44 Detail of Point de Gaze sample from the Spriggs Collection

PART 2

Bridal Accessories

Catherine Barley '90

Tissue Purse with Flower

Pattern 10

Purse

This little purse is intended for a small bridesmaid. It may be worn either diagonally across the body, with the purse at the front, or (with a very short cord) threaded over the sash and worn at the waist.

Materials Required

Brok No. 24 ecru for the cordonnet
No. 30 DMC Machine Broder ecru and 216 peach
Approximately 1 metre of cord for strap (less if to be worn at the waist)
Madeira Decor peach 1514
Small remnant of silk for lining
Small piece of polyester wadding to interline

Back and Front Flap

Using Machine Broder No. 30 ecru, work an open edge round the entire shape (Point d'Espagne). Work the remainder in corded Brussels with four hole diamonds worked at random.

The Cordonnette

Work in peach, using one length of Madeira Decor 1514 doubled. Work the buttonhole stitches in No. 30 DMC Machine Broder peach 216, but make them far enough apart to allow the Madeira Decor to show between them. Work a cordonnette over the inner line

also, using the No. 30 Machine Broder for the buttonhole stitches. Use two lengths of the Machine Broder doubled (four strands), instead of the Madeira Decor.

Purse Front

Work as for the back, with an open-edge border round the sides. There is no need to work a border across the top, as it will be covered by the front flap. Work the two outside edge cordonnettes in the contrast colour as for the back and the front flap. Work the radiating cordonnettes also in the contrast colour, using two lengths of No. 30 Machine Broder doubled instead of Madeira Decor.

To Join Back and Front

1. Remove both pieces from the backing material and place the front of the purse on top of the back, with wrong sides together. Tack the outside edges together and pin the purse to a pillow. This will make it easier to handle.

2. Join the back to the front by working a trefoil edge as you did for the Gros Point sample (pp. 31–3), picking up the edges of both the back and front of the purse. I have joined only the two pieces together in this fashion, but you could also work round the edge of the front flap.

3. Remove the purse from the pillow and take out the tacking stitches. Line and interline the purse and attach required length of cord. I have made a Japanese Kumihimo braid for the purse, using the same threads as for my filling stitches, but a twisted braid would work equally well.

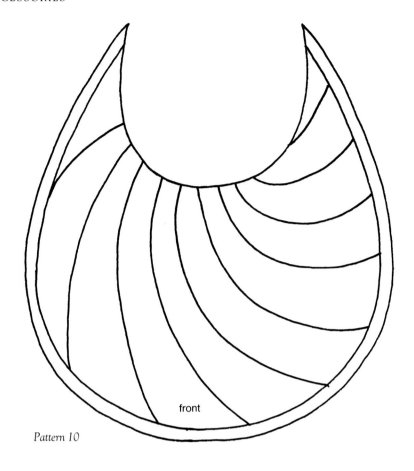

Pattern 10

front

Previous page: Tissue purse and ballet shoes designed and
worked by the author. (Patterns 10 and 11)

120

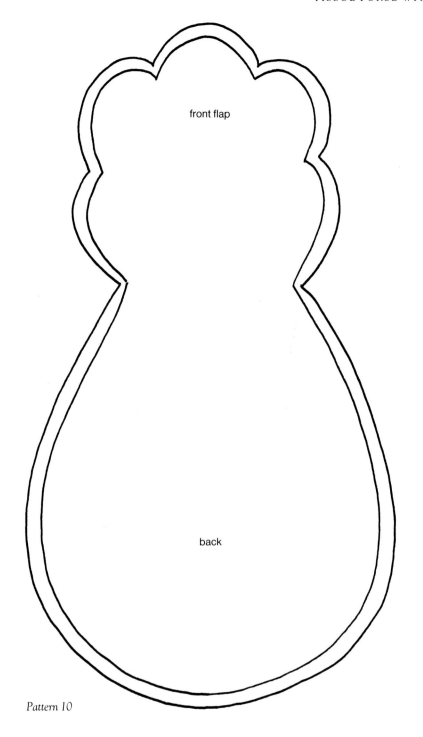

front flap

back

Pattern 10

Pattern 11
Three-Dimensional Flower

A small flower was made in the contrasting colour and attached to the front flap of the purse. The same flower worked in ecru was stitched to tiny peach-coloured ballet shoes to complete the accessories (colour plate, pp. 118–19). The flowers would also look very pretty attached to hairpins and combs, or to an Alice band. The leaves are optional – work in corded Brussels if required.

Materials Required

Brok No. 24 for the cordonnet
DMC Machine Broder No. 30
Madeira Decor
A few small beads for stamens
Fine florist's wire or horsehair

Petals

Make five, working an open edge (Point d'Espagne) with corded Brussels and a four hole diamond.

Couronnes for the Centres

These are worked with a twisted buttonhole stitch round the inside of the central space. Position these stitches where you wish to place the couronnes. Five, I think, will be all that you will have room for.

1. I prefer to work my stitches the Belgian way (upside down), so have started at **A** in diagram 125 and worked round to **B**. If you prefer to work the stitches the other way up (Point d'Espagne) then start at **B** and work round to **A**. All future reference to stitches used in this way will be to 'open edge' stitches to avoid confusion and lengthy explanations. Choose whichever method you prefer.

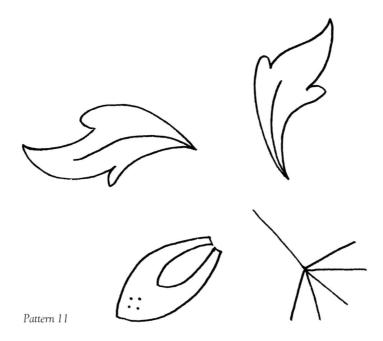

Pattern 11

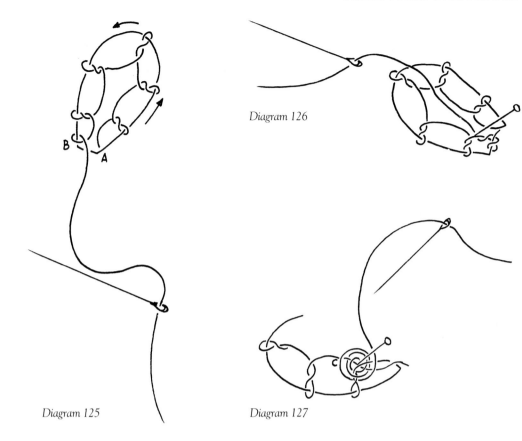

Diagram 126

Diagram 125

Diagram 127

2. Whip back into the first loop and insert a pin close to the first stitch. (Diagram 126)

3. Make a woven wheel by working round the pin, taking the working thread over and under the horizontal and vertical threads. Three or four times should be sufficient, but the gauge of thread and size required will, of course, vary. (Diagram 127)

4. Remove the pin and work buttonhole stitches over the woven wheel. Start at **C** so that you finish back at **C**. Join the ring as you did for the Gros Point sample by slipping into the first stitch made. Whip into the next loop. Repeat for all couronnes.

The Cordonnette

Work as you did for the tissue purse, using a doubled length of Madeira Decor and one length of fine wire (or a doubled length of horsehair).

Stamens

Using Brok No. 24, couch down the central stem and five stamens.

1. Take a length of wire (or horsehair doubled) approximately 14 in. long and, starting at the base of the stem, whip into position up the stem and along the first stamen. Slip a bead onto the wire (or horsehair) and take the working thread and wire through the bead. Bend the wire over and buttonhole stitch back down the stamen over the two lengths of wire, as far as the base of the stamen (diagram 128). *Do not work down the stem.*

2. Work the remaining stamens as for the first, but on completion of the last one, continue to

123

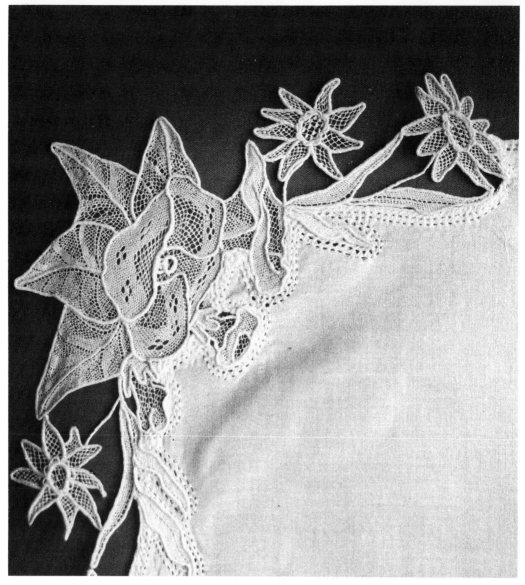

45 Wedding handkerchief designed and worked by Nina
Devereux

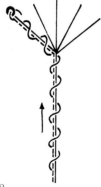

Diagram 128

buttonhole stitch on down the central stem.
Any remaining thread can be left to stitch onto
your chosen accessory.

To Assemble

Stitch all petals together, overlapping the
bottom edges to form a fan shape. Lay the
stamens in the centre. Wrap the petals round
the stamens and close remaining opening.
Gather the bottom edge of the flower to fit and
stitch into position through the stamens.

Coronet and Shoe Rosettes

Pattern 12
Coronet

Materials Required

Brok cotton No. 24 for cordonnet
Brok cotton No. 100/3 or Dragonfly 140
Millinery wire for bottom band
Fine wire or horsehair for stiffening
Roller-blind fabric stiffener

Scrolls

Work as for the scrolls in the Point de Gaze section, working a small diamond as indicated. (Diagram 129)

Central Flower

This is the same flower that was worked for the first Point de Gaze project (pattern 4), but without the bottom petal.

Diagram 129

Top three petals

Work with two rows of open edge, then fill with corded Brussels and small diamonds.

Right- and left-hand petals

Work with one row of open edge and use the shading method covered in pattern 5 (Point de Gaze flower spray, pp. 66–71).

The couronnes

These have one round of open edge worked, then the couronnes are completed in the customary manner. Refer to diagrams 89 and 90 in pattern 6 (p. 78), but note that it will be necessary to whip back round the whole of the wheel.

Small Flowers

Work one row of open edge, whip back and work one row of single Brussels. The remainder of the petal is left open (as for the scalloped scroll, pattern 8, p. 88 and photograph 31).

Flower Couronnes

These are worked separately and stab stitched onto the flowers after the cordonnette has been worked (see Gros Point sample, pattern 1, p. 39).

Leaves

Work one half in corded Brussels and the other in twisted buttonhole stitch without a whipped return (net stitch).

Pattern 12

extra petals

Pattern 12

Bottom Band

Work in corded Brussels, and buttonhole stitch over millinery wire for the cordonnette.

The Cordonnette

Work incorporating fine wire or horsehair to stiffen.

To Complete

1. Stab stitch extra petals to main flower.

2. Remove from backing.

3. Apply one coat of fabric stiffener if required.

4. Bend band round small circular container to shape.

Previous page: Bridal coronet designed and worked by the author. (Pattern 12)

Pattern 13
Shoe Rosette

Materials Required

DMC Machine Broder No. 30
Madeira Decor
Small quantity of beads
Fine wire for stiffening
Roller-blind fabric stiffener

Work in Pea stitch variation No. 3a (Hills & Gibson) along the length of the pattern, threading beads at random onto the loop of the picots. Due to the length of the rows, it will be necessary to renew the working thread in the middle of a row. This is done using the method described for the Hollie Point insertion (p. 46).

46 The same pattern worked with different fillings could be scattered over a bridal veil; designed and worked by the author

Pea Stitch Variation 3a

Work a foundation row of evenly spaced stitches, working from left to right.

Row 1. Worked from right to left. *Work four stitches, miss four loops. Repeat from * to end of row.

Row 2. Worked from left to right. Into the first group of three loops, * work one stitch into the first loop, a loop picot into the second loop, and one stitch into the third loop. Work five stitches into the large loop. Repeat from * to end of row, slipping a small bead onto the working thread as required before you work the loop picot, so that it falls at the bottom of the loop. The picot can be worked following diagram 130a *or* diagram 130b (p. 132).

Row 3. Repeat row 1, working four stitches into the four loops formed in the large loop of the previous row.

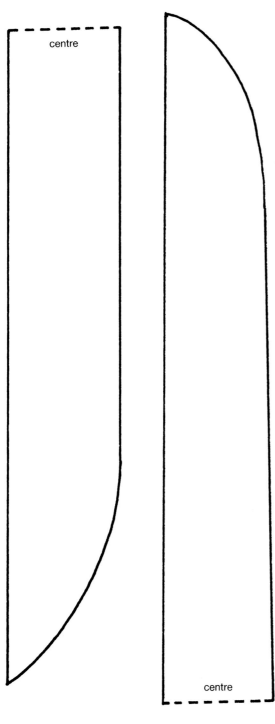

centre

centre

Pattern 13   enlarge by 25%

Bridal shoe rosette designed and worked by the author, with wedding dress panel designed and worked by Jennifer O'Leary. (Pattern 13)

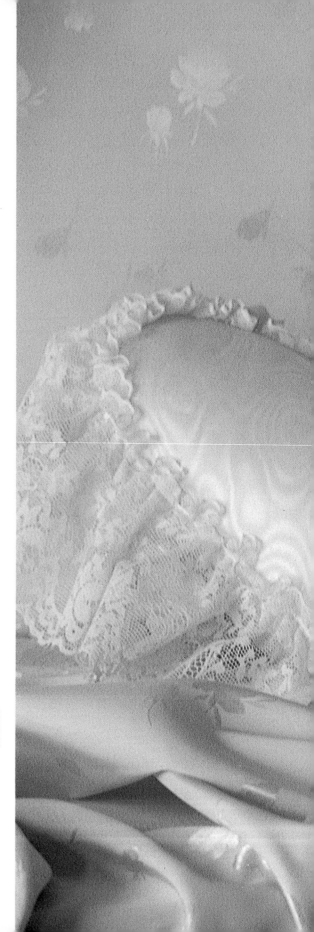

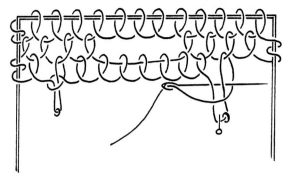

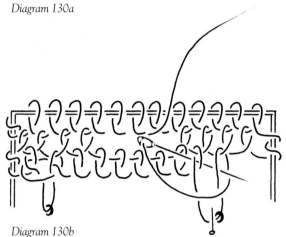

Diagram 130a

Diagram 130b

Row 4. Repeat row 2. The holes and loop picots should alternate like bricks, as in other Pea stitch fillings. (Diagrams 130a and b)

If you find it too difficult to work such long rows, then work across the short length of the shape. It will, however, be necessary to choose another filling stitch, because the looped picot will be sideways on, and the weight of the bead will pull it to one side.

1. Work an open edge from **A** to **B**, then whip back and work a foundation row. This is the top edge of the rosette. (Diagram 131)

2. Work three-quarters of the way down the shape, work three or four rows of corded Brussels, then two pattern repeats of the Pea stitch. Finally work the remaining area in corded Brussels.

3. When the whole area has been completed and *before* working the cordonnette, lightly spray with one coat of roller-blind stiffener and allow to dry thoroughly. This will prevent the large area of filling stitches from collapsing.

4. Work a cordonnette along the sides and top straight edge from **C–D**, over a doubled length of Madeira Decor and one length of fine wire. (Diagram 131)

5. Remove the work from its backing and make a double row of running stitches from **E–F**. (Diagram 132)

Diagram 131

Diagram 132

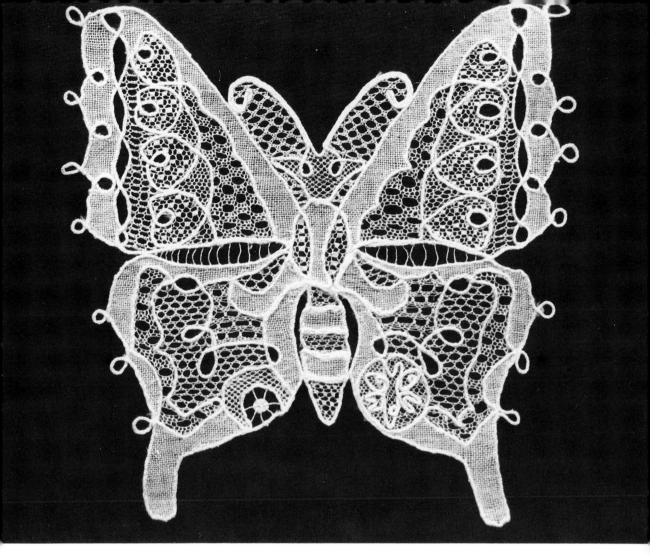

47 Halas lace butterfly worked by Marie Laurie of New
South Wales, Australia

6. Pull up the threads to gather the curved
edge, until approximately 13 cm. (5 in.) in
length. (Diagram 133)

7. Roll from one end to form a rosette, sewing
the gathered edges together as you roll the lace.

8. Bend the wired edge to form a naturalistic
flower. When you are satisfied with the

formation, spray once more with the roller-
blind fabric stiffener and allow to dry
completely before attaching to your chosen
accessory.

Several rosettes could be used on a hairband,
and a single one on a hairpin or haircomb, with
perhaps a few leaves and ribbons added to
complete the arrangement. In the section at
the back of this book are extra patterns
incorporating some of the scrolls previously
covered in Part I. You might like to try one of
these, choosing your own filling stitches or
perhaps adding the bride's initials or the date of
the wedding to personalise the project.

Diagram 133

133

PART 3

Contemporary Projects

Three-Dimensional Strawberries

Pattern 14

These three-dimensional strawberries make an unusual gift, perhaps for a ruby wedding.

Materials Required

Fine black wire or black stamens (legs of bee)
Fine green florist's wire and small gold beads
Gütermann silks 100/3 green shades 921, 432, 841 (leaves and stems)
Red shades 384 and 909 (strawberries)
Green 432 and 582 (unripe strawberry and young fruit)
Grey 701, gold 416, brown 817, black (bee)
Fine Honiton thread 120 and gold aerosol paint (wings)
Unity 150 or Dragonfly 140 (flowers)
Cream 325 (flower centres)
Small amount of soft-toy stuffing

Cordonnet

Use a doubled length of 100/3 silk for all pattern pieces; this should be the same colour as for the fillings.

Strawberries

You will need to make four strawberries altogether – three red and a small one in green. Two pattern shapes are required for each (a back and a front).

1. Using red shade 384, work corded Brussels diagonally across the pattern piece. (Diagram 134)

Strawberries

Pattern 14

2. When the whole area is completed work Pea stitch variation No. 3a (Hills & Gibson) over the top of the corded Brussels, using red shade 909, as worked for the shoe rosette in the previous pattern (diagrams 130a and b, p. 132). Thread gold beads at random onto the loop picots. This is one of those occasions when the stitch must be worked from top to bottom of the strawberry, otherwise the weight of the bead might turn the picot upside down. (Diagram 135)

Calyx

Work in corded Brussels, using green shade 921 and working short rows as required (indicated on pattern). No stiffening is required in the cordonnette, just buttonhole stitch round the edge to neaten.

137

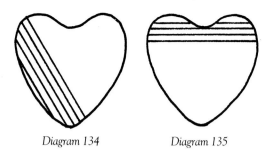

Diagram 134   Diagram 135

Stems

Work the small circular shape at the top in corded Brussels, using green shade 921. Start at **A** in diagram 136 with a single length of wire and buttonhole stitch up the stem to **B**. Continue round the top and back to **B**. Cut off the wire but leave any small length of thread, as this will be tucked inside the strawberry.

To Assemble

Place right sides of the strawberry together and join by slip stitching the edges from **A** to **B**

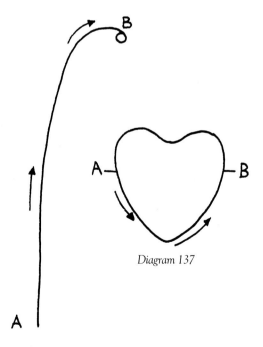

Diagram 137

Diagram 136

(diagram 137). Turn the strawberry inside out and stuff firmly with soft-toy stuffing, leaving sufficient space to insert the circular end of the stem. Finally add a little more stuffing (a pair of tweezers is useful) and complete the stitching, taking the needle back and forth through the small circular area at the end of the stem. This will prevent the stem from slipping out of the strawberry.

Place the calyx round the stem and position over the top of the strawberry. Secure with a few stitches. Make one small green strawberry using the darker shade of green 432 for the corded Brussels, and shade 581 for the Pea stitch.

Strawberry Leaves

The leaves of the strawberry plant have a very textured appearance with many veins and little space between them for the filling stitches. I found the easiest way to achieve this effect was to work the leaves without couching down the veins. A selection of shades of green has been given. You can use them all, just one or two, or work them all the same.

Work rows of corded Brussels diagonally (diagram 138). Working the rows in this direction makes it easier to work the many small areas along the outside edges of the leaves. You will notice that the rows are worked closer together towards the central vein, and further apart towards the edge of the leaf. Pull the stitches tight towards the vein (making them shorter), and make them longer towards the edge of the leaf.

When you have filled in all three leaves on the stem, work round the edge of each leaf with a doubled length of 100/3 silk for the cordonnette. It is not necessary to wire the outside edge, as there will be sufficient support in the many veins that have to be worked. It would also be difficult to bend the wire round the many tiny sharp bends. Work the cordonnette round all three leaves, leaving only the veins and stems to be wired.

Three-Dimensional Strawberries. Designed and worked
by the author. (Pattern 14)

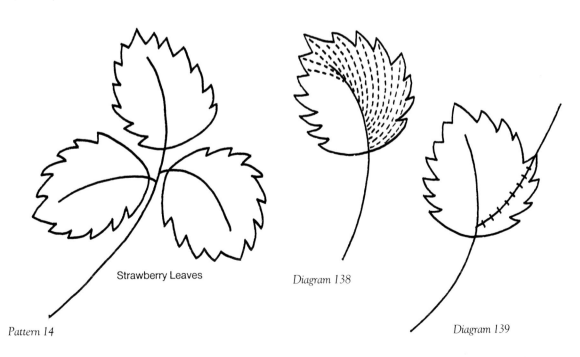

Strawberry Leaves

Diagram 138

Pattern 14

Diagram 139

To Work the Veins

Take a length of fine florist's wire and bend it into a gentle curve. Lay the wire on the leaf and slip stitch it into position (diagram 139). Cut off the excess wire on the diagonal (this makes it easier to cover the ends) and buttonhole stitch over the wire with the straight edge of the buttonhole stitch on the outside edge of the curve.

Work the veins for all three leaves, leaving the central veins of each leaf, and the stems, until the very last. This will make handling far easier.

To Work the Central Veins and Stem

Start at the top of the leaf and slip stitch the wire into position. Buttonhole stitch down this central vein and stem until the next leaf is reached. When the stem from this leaf joins the main stem from the first one, proceed to buttonhole stitch over the two wires.

Repeat again with the third leaf, working over the three wires for the main stem until approximately 1 cm. before the end. Cut off one wire on the diagonal, work a few more stitches then cut off a second wire. Work almost to the tip of the stem, then cut off the remaining wire. It is easier to cover the ends of the wire by cutting them off one at a time than to cut off all three at once.

Make as many sprays of leaves as required to create your own arrangement.

Flowers

Each flower has five petals worked in corded Brussels, with an open edge (see pattern 4, diagram 54, p. 56). Each petal incorporates fine wire or horsehair in the cordonnette. Work in Unity 150 or Dragonfly 140.

The stems and calyx

These are worked as for the strawberry stem and calyx, using green shade 582 (see pp. 137–8). Make three. Each has one flower at the top and two young fruit.

Flower centres

Work the circular shapes in corded Brussels, using cream shade 325. Before you remove them from the backing material, make tiny french knots in cream 325 in the centre and Venetian picots (see Gros Point, p. 33) 2 mm. in from the outside edge, in gold shade 416. *Do not work them through the backing material.*

To assemble the flowers

Stitch the petals together, overlapping at the bottom to form a fan shape. Slip one calyx onto each stem. Make running stitches round the small circular area and gather up. Stuff with wadding and insert the stem into the centre. Stitch into position as you did for the strawberries.

Place the fan shape of petals round the stem. Close final opening and stitch to stamens, gathering the bottom edge to fit. Push the calyx up to the back of the flower and stitch into position.

Young Fruit

Make two. Work in corded Brussels using green 582. Work two of the egg-cosy shapes and two calyces for each fruit.

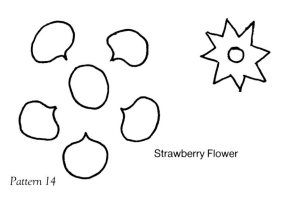

Strawberry Flower

Pattern 14

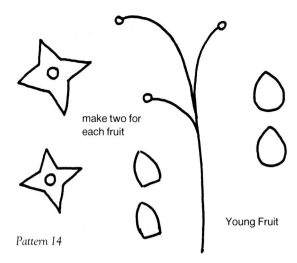

make two for
each fruit

Young Fruit

Pattern 14

Stitch the two pieces together, leaving the bottom edge open. Stuff as for the strawberries. Slip the calyx into position as for the strawberries, placing first the larger of the two, then the smaller one.

To assemble the fruits

Insert the stem into the fruit and stitch into position as for the strawberries. Gather the bottom edge of the fruit and close. Push up each of the calyces and stitch into position, alternating the points.

The Bee

You may find you need to work more rows or less, depending on your tension. Start at the head and work in corded Brussels.

1. Two rows grey stitching 701 over grey cord.

2. One row grey stitching 701 over yellow cord 416.

3. Two rows yellow stitching over yellow cord 416.

4. One row brown stitching 817 over yellow cord 416.

5. One row brown stitching over brown cord 817.

6. Work rows of black stitching over brown cord until just before the centre of the body.

7. Two rows yellow stitching over brown cord.

8. One row brown over yellow cord.

9. Black over brown until halfway down tail section.

10. One row yellow over brown.

11. One row yellow over yellow.

12. One row black over yellow.

13. One row white over black.

Finally work white over white to the end. Work a second shape in brown for the underside of the bee.

Wings

Make four. I could not find a metallic thread fine enough to get the effect I wanted. After trying four different makes of thread, and even splitting some of them, I found the best result I could achieve was using 120 Honiton thread worked in single Brussels stitch.

Wire the outside edge of the wings, using fine florist's wire or horsehair for the cordonnette. Remove the wings from the backing material and spray lightly with gold paint.

To assemble the bee

Stitch both halves of the bee together, leaving a small opening. Stuff with soft-toy stuffing and close the opening. Stitch the wings in position and cut small lengths of black stamens for the legs and antennae. Work french knots or use tiny black beads for the eyes.

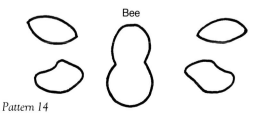

Bee

Pattern 14

141

Peapods with Butterfly

Who would have thought that the kitchen garden would be a source of inspiration for a project? These peapods seem to have a great appeal and would make an ideal gift for a friend or relative who enjoys gardening. The butterfly could be worked on its own and attached to a brooch mount. Another alternative would be to make two pea flowers and a bud on each stem, and work several sprays in sweet-pea colours. The same-size pattern will also work for the sweet peas.

Pattern 15a
Peapods

Materials Required

Fine green florist's wire
Small amount of soft-toy stuffing
Size 14 (2 mm.) knitting needle
Gütermann 100/3 silk in green shades 283, 432, 582, 921
Unity 150 or Dragonfly 140 white

Peapods

Work in corded Brussels lengthwise, as indicated on the pattern. Only the curved front edge of the large pod need be wired. Use shade 283. Incorporate one length of fine green florist's wire when working the cordonnette. The two smaller pods need no wire.

Calyx

This is also in corded Brussels. Work short rows

as indicated on the pattern, when required, using shade 432. The calyces need not be wired, just buttonhole stitch round the edge to neaten. You will need one calyx for each pod.

Peas

Make six, using shade 582. Work in corded Brussels.

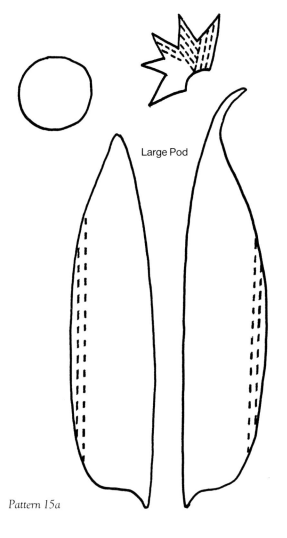

Large Pod

Pattern 15a

142

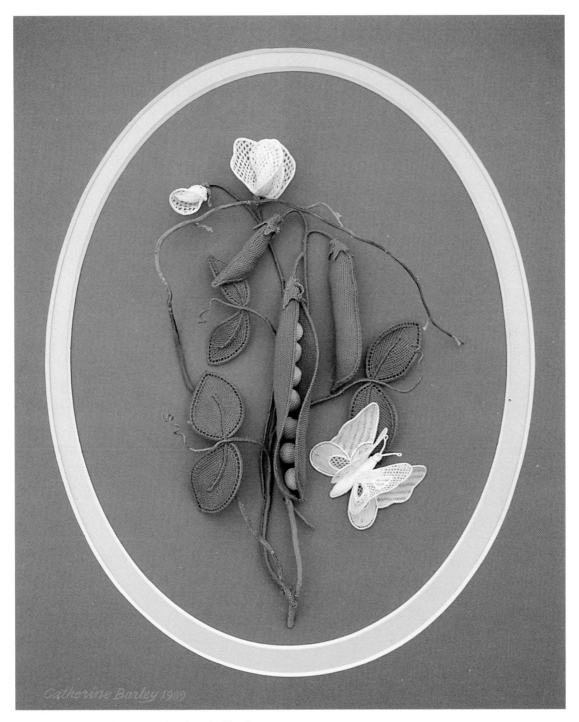

Peapods with Butterfly. Designed and worked by the
author. (Pattern 15)

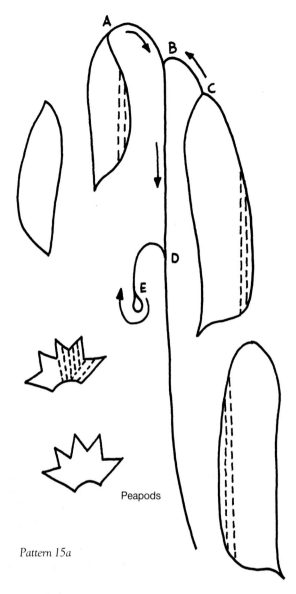

Peapods

Pattern 15a

extending into the pod. Buttonhole stitch up to **B**.

2. Work over both wires to **D** and leave.

3. Start at **E** with a third length of wire, work round the small circle and up the stem to **D**.

4. Work over the three wires until 1 cm. (⅜ in.) from the end. Cut off one wire diagonally, work two or three stitches. Cut off the second wire and repeat. Finally cut off the third wire. Any working thread remaining can be left and taken through the backing material when you finally mount the pieces.

To assemble the large pod

1. Stitch the two sections together down the back spine only.

2. Make small running stitches round the outside edge of the peas and gather up. Stuff with wadding and stitch into position down the centre of the pod.

3. Insert the wire into the pod and secure with a few stitches into the small circle to prevent the wire coming out of the pod.

4. Wrap the calyx round the wire at the top of the pod and stitch into position.

5. Join both halves of the two smaller pods, leaving a small opening to stuff. Close the opening. Position calyx and stitch to secure.

The stems

For the bottom stem (without a peapod) work the small circle in corded Brussels, using shade 283.

1. Lay a length of green wire over the top of the stem at **A**, leaving approximately 1 cm. of wire extending into the pod. Buttonhole stitch over this wire to **B**, where it joins the main stem, and leave. (There is no need to buttonhole over the wire extending into the pod.) Lay another length of wire over the next stem at **C**, again leaving 1 cm. of wire

The Flower

You will need to make one flower and one bud, using Unity 150 or Dragonfly 140.

1. Work the small bean-shaped pieces in corded Brussels as indicated on the pattern. These need not be wired.

2. The flower petals are worked in Pea stitch (Gros Point, pp. 13–14), as indicated by the dotted lines on the pattern, with the small sections at the base worked in corded Brussels.

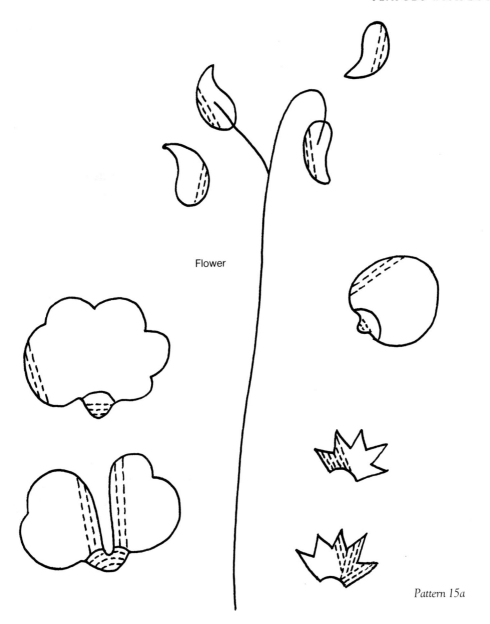

Flower

Pattern 15a

3. Incorporate fine florist's wire round the outside edges of the three petals, but not across the bottom area worked in corded Brussels. This will make it easier to fold the petals for final assembly.

Calyx

Work in corded Brussels, using shade 432. Work as for the pod calyx.

The stem

Work as for the stems of the pea pods, extending a small length of wire into the bud area, which will support the weight of the flower.

To assemble the flower

1. Remove all pieces from the backing material. Bend the length of wire that extends

145

Playmates. The background was painted by Roy Barley
and the stumpwork figures worked by the author.

into the bud area to the other side of the work
(inside the bud) and stitch bean shapes
together, leaving a small opening. Stuff and
close the opening.

2. Fold the divided petal in half and place it
round the bud at the top of the stem, with the
straight edges at the top of the flower. Stitch
into position through the bud.

3. Wrap the larger of the two remaining petals
over the first one to form the flower, and stitch
in position.

4. Wrap the calyx round the base of the flower
and secure with a few stitches.

5. Wrap the remaining petal round the second
bud and complete (see colour plate, p. 143.)

The Leaves

*Couch to the top of the leaves only; do not work
along the dotted line.* Work in corded Brussels,
using shade 921. The veins could be made
open by working the rows diagonally (working
Point d'Espagne into every other stitch), as you
did in the Gros Point sample and also some of
the Point de Gaze samples. They could also be
worked the same way as the strawberry leaves
(p. 138) or couched down initially. I have

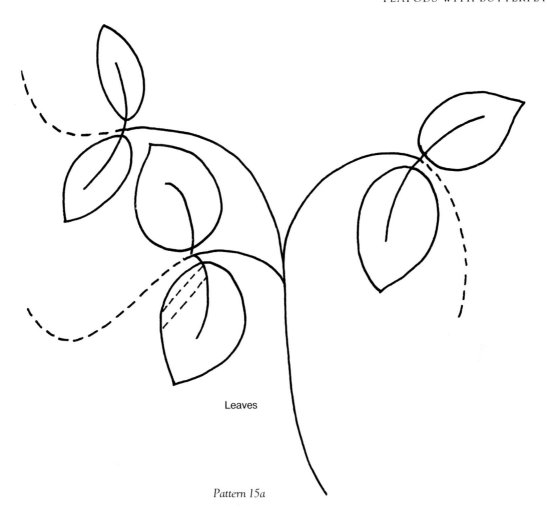

Leaves

Pattern 15a

worked the leaves with an open edge (Point d'Espagne), but have not worked any veins at all. The outside edge of the leaf is stiffened by incorporating wire in the cordonnette.

The stems

These and the central vein in the leaves are worked as for the flower stems, leaving a length of wire extending beyond the two leaves. *Do not buttonhole stitch over this length of wire*, but when you have removed the spray of leaves from its backing, wrap the wire round a size 14 (2 mm.) knitting needle to form the tendril.

Pattern 15b
Butterfly

Materials Required

Horsehair or fine wire
Egyptian cotton No. 160
If the Egyptian cotton 160 is too fine for your
eyesight, then choose any thread used for
Honiton that you feel happy with. However, if
you use a thicker thread you will obviously
work less rows.

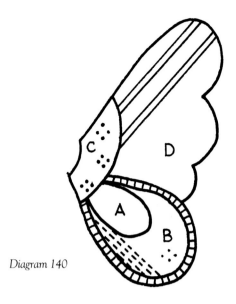

Diagram 140

Body

Work in corded Brussels, using fine wire or
incorporating horsehair for the antennae (as
for the flower petals). Stitch the two halves
together and stuff.

Pattern 15b

Large Wings

Refer to diagram 140.
Area A. Pea stitch (See Gros Point section,
pp. 13–14)
Area B. Open edge (see Point d'Espagne,
p. 41) and corded Brussels with a four hole
diamond
Area C. Work as for area **B**, but making
several four hole diamonds at random.
Area D. Work three rows of corded Brussels,
alternating with two rows of Point d'Espagne
worked in pairs to form a V-shape. If you are
using a thicker thread you may need to adjust
the number of rows, i.e. by working two rows
of corded Brussels and one row Point
d'Espagne.

Small Wings

Refer to diagram 141.
Area E. Corded Brussels with a four hole
diamond and open edge.
Area F. Open edge and only one row of corded
Brussels. Centre left open.
Area G. Open edge – three rows corded
Brussels – open edge – and Rosebud knots.
(See pattern 5, diagrams 84–86, p. 72.)
Area H. Pea stitch

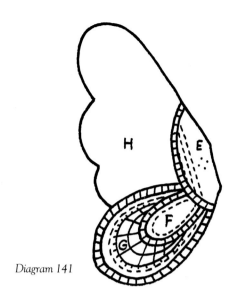

Diagram 141

To Assemble

Stitch the wings in position either side of the body, attaching the large wings first and the smaller wings on the top. Assemble all pieces to form a pleasing arrangement.

The Promise of Spring

Pattern 16

These three-dimensional daffodils and
primroses would make an ideal gift for a golden
wedding anniversary. I have done my best to
reproduce them as accurately as possible, and
have tried to convey the different varieties by
using a different filling stitch for each of them.
The petals could be pale lemon with trumpets
the colour of egg yolks, or you could make
some petals and trumpets gold, whilst others
might be white with just a hint of lemon. I
worked the whole of my arrangement in white,
mounting it in a gold frame against a mustard-
coloured background.

Materials Required

Fine florist's wire or horsehair
Brok cotton No. 24 for the cordonnet
Dragonfly 140 or Brok 100/3
Size 8 mm. knitting needle
Small beads for stamens
If you would prefer to work in colour then try
one strand of embroidery cotton, sewing cotton
or Madeira Tanne 30 or 80. If you find that
these threads are too fine to work with, try
enlarging the pattern and using thicker thread.

The Daffodils

You will need to make six petals. The dotted
line in the pattern indicates the angle and
direction of the rows, and also the starting
place. I have worked one flower in simple
corded Brussels with a four hole diamond and
an open edge for each of the petals (Point
d'Espagne), and the other in Inverted Pyramid
stitch. (Diagram 142)

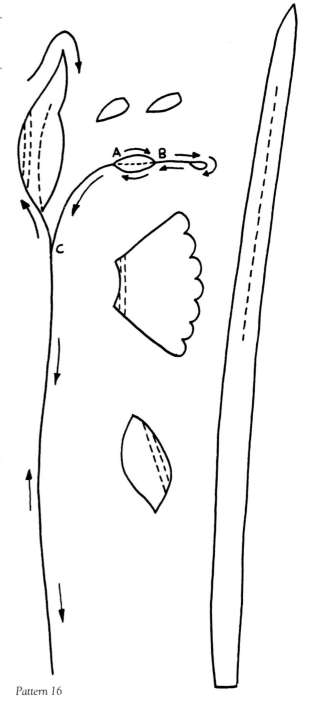

Pattern 16

The Promise of Spring. Designed and worked by the
author. (Pattern 16)

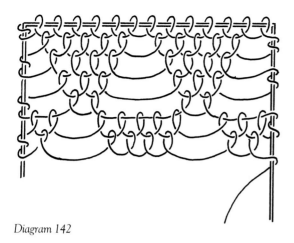

Diagram 142

Inverted pyramids

Make a foundation row of evenly spaced stitches.

Row 1. *Make one stitch into each of the first five loops, miss one loop. *Repeat from * to end of row.*

Row 2. *Miss one loop, make one stitch into each of the next four loops, and repeat from * to the end of the row.

Row 3. *Miss one loop, make one stitch into each of the next three loops. Repeat from * to end of row.

Row 4. *Miss one loop, make one stitch into each of the next two loops. Repeat from * to end of row.

Row 5. You can see that the groups of stitches gradually decrease to form a triangle, and that the gap between these triangles gradually becomes larger. This next row is the same as the first, in that you *make five stitches into the large loop, miss one loop and repeat from * to the end of the row.

The cordonnette

Work using two strands of the same thread used for filling stitches and one length of fine florist's wire.

Trumpet

Start at the base, perhaps with a different filling stitch from that used for the petals. I have worked one trumpet in corded Brussels with four hole diamonds made at random. The other I have worked with two rows of corded Brussels then two pattern repeats of Pea stitch, but worked in the opposite direction. It is only necessary to stiffen the top and bottom of the trumpet, as the sides will have to be joined to form a cone shape. Buttonholed loops can be used to create the frilly effect on the top edge, but if you are using wire, you could do this by pinching the wire at intervals with a small pair of pliers.

To join the trumpet

Wrap round a large knitting needle (size 8 mm.) and join along the straight edge with a flat seam to form a cone shape. The flowers are not difficult to make but you do need nimble fingers to assemble them.

To work the stem

Couch down the cordonnet in the usual way. Work the leaf shape and small oval shape on the branching bar in corded Brussels.

The cordonnette

Start at **A** in the pattern diagram, using two strands of thread doubled and one length of florist's wire. Work to the base of the stamen **B** and then whip down the strand of wire. Thread a bead onto the wire and bend it over to form a loop. Proceed to buttonhole stitch back down the stem, working round the oval shape and on down until you reach the main stem at **C**. Whip the threads and wire down to the base of the main stem, fold back the threads and wire and buttonhole stitch back up the main stem. Continue round the leaf shape and finish by cutting off the cordonnette threads. Leave the working thread if it is long enough, as this can be used to assemble the flower.

Pattern 16

The oval sections are stitched together to form a pyramid shape, leaving one seam open to enable you to stuff and close it.

To assemble the flower

Insert the stamen into the trumpet of the daffodil and stitch in place, making sure that the calyx (oval shape) is left outside the trumpet. Stitch the remaining petals into position to make up the flower.

Leaves

Work in corded Brussels with an open vein down the centre, as indicated on the pattern.

Primroses

Work five petals for each flower. The stem and calyx are worked as for the daffodils. On completion, stitch the two halves of the calyx together and stuff. Stitch the petals together to form a fan shape by overlapping the bottom edges. Place the petals round the stem and sew in position. Wrap the sepals round the calyx and stitch in place.

Leaves

Work in corded Brussels with four hole diamonds, working the rows diagonally as indicated on the pattern. Make as many as required for your own arrangement.

153

The Gardenia

Pattern 17

This small spray of gardenias would make an ideal gift for Mother's Day, or a birthday present for a special aunt or friend. It is very simple to make and I have used Pea stitch for the flowers (as used in the Gros Point sample, diagram 3, p. 14) with corded Brussels for the leaves, incorporating open veins. The veins could, of course, be couched down initially and worked with a cordonnette to give a raised effect, as for the central vein and the strawberries in pattern 14 (p.137). For the large flower you will need six large petals and five small ones. For the small flower you will need to make around five small petals.

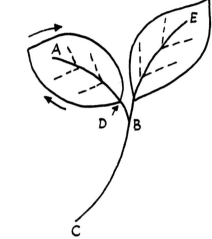

Diagram 143

Materials Required

Brok cotton No. 24 for cordonnet
Brok cotton 100/3 for the filling stitches
Fine wire for stiffening
Small amount of cotton wool for stuffing

Filling Stitches

Leaves

The leaves are worked in corded Brussels with open veins. (Diagram 143)

Flowers

The petals are worked in Pea stitch (or a stitch or your own choice).

The three small bud sections are worked in corded Brussels.

To Wire and Work the Cordonnette

1. Take one length of 100/3 doubled and one length of fine wire, and buttonhole stitch down the central stem and vein from **A** to **B** in diagram 143.

2. Whip down the remainder of the wire to the bottom of the stem, then cut off the surplus wire, but leave the working thread.

3. Start with a fresh wire and a doubled length of thread at **D**, and proceed to work round the outside edge of the leaf and back to **D**. (Start with the wire extending approximately 3½ cm. (1 in.) and when you have worked sufficient stitches and are sure that the wire is secure,

The Gardenia. Designed and worked by the author. (Pattern 17)

154

bud sections (make three)

bud sections (make three)

Petals and sepals

Pattern 17

gently pull the other end so that the extended wire just disappears under the first stitch, as you did in the Gros Point sample, p. 28. This is far easier than trying to make the wire the correct length to start with.) Cut off the remaining wire as close as possible, taking care not to cut the working thread.

4. Start at **C** with one wire and a doubled length of thread, using the thread that was left behind at the base of the stem as the working thread (you will be working over two wires and two threads). Keep the edge of the buttonhole stitch on the outside of the curve, and work right up the main stem and remaining threads

156

to **E** (diagram 143), reversing the edge of the buttonhole stitches as the curve changes. Cut off the wire at the top and secure the working thread. Work the second leaf in the same way as the first.

Stem for flower and central bud

The small oval shape at the top is worked in corded Brussels. (Diagram 144)

1. Start at **A** with one wire and a doubled length of thread. Work up the stem to **B**, then round the top and back to **B**. Cut off the remaining wire and secure the working thread. (Diagram 144)

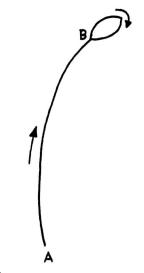

Diagram 144

2. Start at **A** (the bud at the top of the stem) with one length of wire and a doubled length of thread. Work round the loop to **B** and continue down the stem to **C** and leave. (Diagram 145)

3. Start at the top of the vein **D** with one wire and one length of doubled thread, and work down the stem to join the other wire at **C**. Keep the straight edge of the buttonhole stitches on the outside of the curve: this will require reversing the direction of the stitch halfway down the stem. Work over both sets of thread and wire, down to the base of the stem. Cut off the wire. If you are going to frame the spray, the working thread could be left and taken through the backing material when mounted. If not, secure and cut off.

4. Start at **E** (edge of leaf) with the same number of threads and wire, and work right round the leaf, back to **E**. Cut off. (Diagram 145)

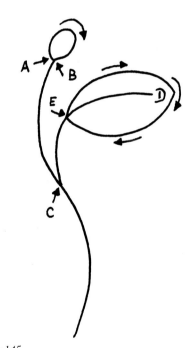

Diagram 145

The three bud sections

1. No wire need be used for these three sections. Start at **A** in diagram 146 with two threads doubled (four threads) and work round to **B**. Do not work across the base.

2. Remove the three sections from the backing

Diagram 146

material and stitch together, using a fine thread, through the loops of the cordonnette stitches, to form a pyramid or egg-cosy shape. The base is left open.

To Assemble the Flowers

Remove all pieces from the backing. Wrap cotton wool round each of the buds at the top of the stems, shaping to resemble a bud, then insert the padded end of the stem into the pyramid which was made up of the three bud sections. This is a little difficult, and a pair of tweezers will help. Run a thread round the base of the pyramid and pull up to close the base.

Place each petal one at a time around this bud, and stitch into position. You can stitch right through the cotton-wool-filled bud if necessary. Form to make a pleasing arrangement.

Swan with Raised Wings

Pattern 18

Materials Required

Unity 150 or Dragonfly 140
Horsehair or fine wire for wings

The whole of the swan is worked in corded Brussels, with an open edge to the neck and body.

1. Work an open edge from the beak to the tail end and whip back. Work both top and bottom edges of the swan.

2. The first row is worked from **A** to **B** or **B** to **A**, depending on which way you prefer to

Swan with Raised Wings. Designed and worked by the author. (Pattern 18)

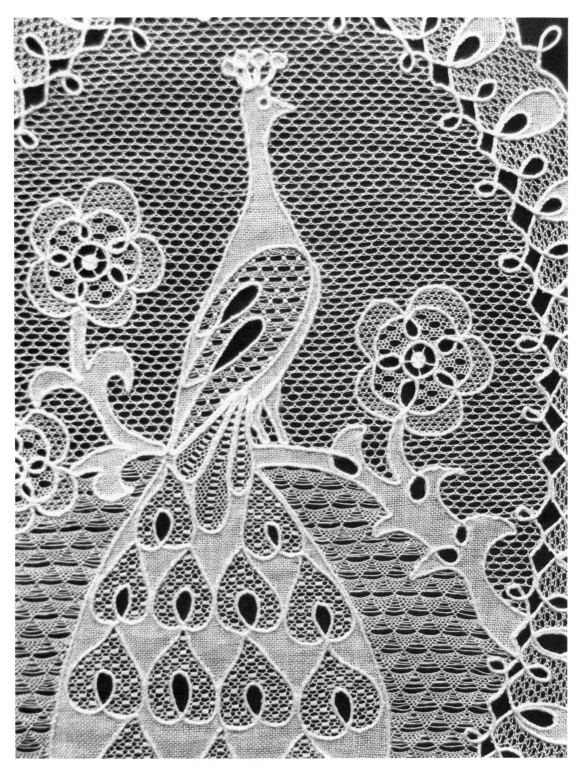

48 Peacock detail from an oval mat of Halas lace. The cloth-like areas are not of fabric, but horizontal and vertical threads woven with needle and thread by the worker.

Pattern 18

work. Progress up the body, working open veins towards the tail end. This creates a feathered effect to the tail.

3. Work the wings in Inverted Pyramid stitch as for the daffodils in the previous project (diagram 142, p. 152). Wing 4 indicates the direction and position of the first row. Work all wings in this direction.

4. Work the cordonnette for the swan over two lengths of thread doubled. For the wings add one length of fine wire or one length of horsehair doubled.

5. When all sections are complete, remove from the backing and stab stitch the wings into position.

PART 4

Pattern Section

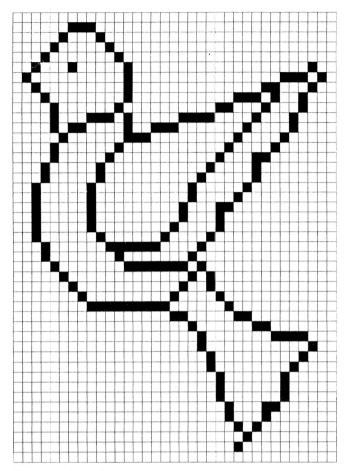

Pattern supplement 1

Pattern supplement 2

Pattern supplement 3

Pattern supplement 4

Pattern supplement 5

Pattern supplement 6

Pattern supplement 7

Pattern supplement 8

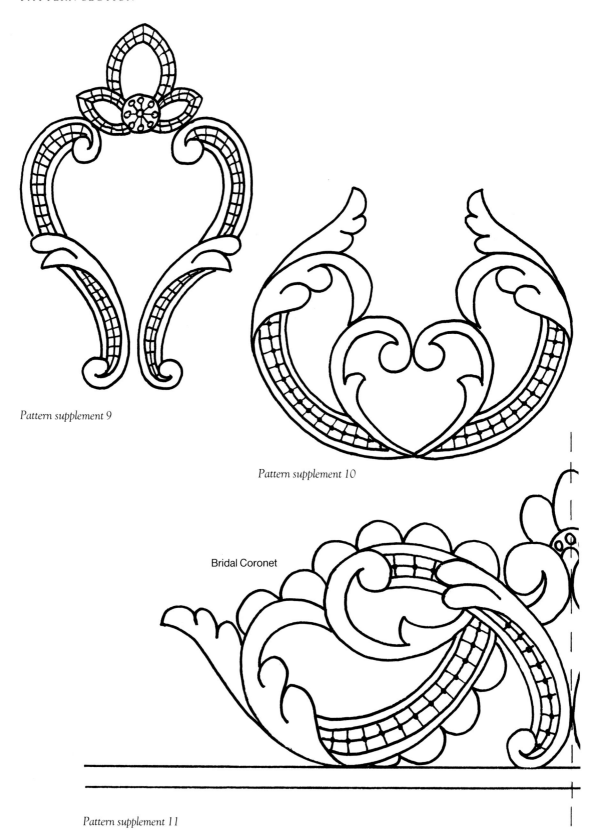

Pattern supplement 9

Pattern supplement 10

Bridal Coronet

Pattern supplement 11

166

Pattern supplement 12

use one on its own
or join two to form a ring

Pattern supplement 13

Pattern supplement 14

Pattern supplement 15

Pattern supplement 16

Pattern supplement 17

Pattern supplement 18

Pattern supplement 19

Tea cosy designed by Marjorie Crump, using the central flower motif from the antique lace shown in photograph 17. Enlarge by 25% for a small teapot or by 75% for a normal-size pot.

Pattern supplement 20

Book Suppliers

ENGLAND
The following are stockists of the Batsford/Dryad Press range:

AVON
Bridge Bookshop
7 Bridge Street
Bath BA2 4AS

Waterstone & Co.
4–5 Milsom Street
Bath BA1 1DA

BEDFORDSHIRE
Arthur Sells
Lane Cover
49 Pedley Lane
Clifton
Shefford SG17 5QT

BUCKINGHAMSHIRE
J.S. Sear
Lacecraft Supplies
8 Hillview
Sherington MK16 9NJ

CAMBRIDGESHIRE
Dillons the Bookstore
Sidney Street
Cambridge

CHESHIRE
Lynn Turner
Church Meadow Crafts
7 Woodford Road
Winsford

DEVON
Creative Crafts & Needlework
18 High Street
Totnes TQ9 5NP

Honiton Lace Shop
44 High Street
Honiton EX14 8PJ

DORSET
F. Herring & Sons
27 High West Street
Dorchester DT1 1UP

Tim Parker (*mail order*)
124 Corhampton Road
Boscombe East
Bournemouth BH6 5NZ

Christopher Williams
19 Morrison Avenue
Parkstone
Poole BH17 4AD

DURHAM
Lacemaid
6, 10 & 15 Stoneybeck
Bishop Middleham DL17 9BL

GLOUCESTERSHIRE
Southgate Handicrafts
63 Southgate Street
Gloucester GL1 1TX

Waterstone & Company
89–90 The Promenade
Cheltenham GL50 1NB

HAMPSHIRE
Creative Crafts
11 The Square
Winchester SO23 9ES

Doreen Gill
14 Barnfield Road
Petersfield GU31 4DR

Needlestyle
24–26 West Street
Alresford

Ruskins
27 Bell Street
Romsey

ISLE OF WIGHT
Busy Bobbins
Unit 7
Scarrots Lane
Newport PO30 1JD

KENT
The Handicraft Shop
47 Northgate
Canterbury CT1 1BE

Hatchards
The Great Hall
Mount Pleasant Road
Tunbridge Wells

LONDON
W. & G. Foyle Ltd
113–119 Charing Cross Road
WC2H 0EB

Hatchards
187 Piccadilly W1V 9DA

MIDDLESEX
Redburn Crafts
Squires Garden Centre
Halliford Road
Upper Halliford
Shepperton TW17 8RU

NORFOLK
Alby Lace Museum
Cromer Road
Alby
Norwich NR11 7QE

Jane's Pincushions
Taverham Craft Unit 4
Taverham Nursery Centre
Fir Covert Road
Taverham
Norwich NR8 6HT

Waterstone & Company Ltd
30 London Street
Norwich NR2 1LD

NORTH YORKSHIRE
Craft Basics
9 Gillygate
York

Shireburn Lace
Finkle Court
Finkle Hill
Sherburn in Elmet LS25 6EB

The Craft House
23 Bar Street
Scarborough YO13 9QE

SOMERSET
Bridge Bookshop
62 Bridge Street
Taunton TA1 1UD

STAFFORDSHIRE
J. & J. Ford (*mail order & lace days only*)
October Hill
Upper Way
Upper Longdon
Rugeley WS15 1QB

SUSSEX
Waterstone & Company Ltd
120 Terminus Road
Eastbourne

WARWICKSHIRE
Christine & David Springett
21 Hillmorton Road
Rugby CV22 6DF

WEST MIDLANDS
Needlewoman
21 Needles Alley
off New Street
Birmingham B2 5AG

WEST YORKSHIRE
Sebalace
Waterloo Mill
Howden Road
Silsden BD20 0HA

George White Lacemaking
   Supplies
40 Heath Drive
Boston Spa LS23 6PB

Just Lace
Lacemaker Supplies
14 Ashwood Gardens
Gildersome
Leeds LS27 7AS

Jo Firth
58 Kent Crescent
Lowtown, Pudsey
Leeds LS28 9EB

WILTSHIRE
Everyman Bookshop
5 Bridge Street
Salisbury SP1 2ND

SCOTLAND
Embroidery Shop
51 William Street
Edinburgh
Lothian EH3 7LW

Waterstone & Company Ltd
236 Union Street
Aberdeen AB1 1TN

WALES
Bryncraft Bobbins (*mail order*)
B.J. Phillips
Pantglas
Cellan
Lampeter
Dyfed SA48 8JD

Hilkar Lace Suppliers
33 Mysydd Road
Landore
Swansea

Sources of Information

Guild of Needlelaces
Mrs June Dawkins
Netherlea
39 Moor Road
Breadsall
Derby DE7 6AA

OIDFA (International Bobbin
   and Needlelace Organization)

President
Kathy Kauffmann
1301 Greenwood
Wilmette
IL 60091
USA

Vice President
Hilary Booth
39 Craigweil Avenue
Radlett
Herts WD7 7ET

The Lace Guild
The Hollies
53 Audnam
Stourbridge
West Midlands DY8 4AE

The Lacemakers' Circle
49 Wardwick
Derby DE1 1HY

The Lace Society
Linwood
Stratford Road
Oversley
Alcester
War BY9 6PG

Equipment Suppliers

See also **Book Suppliers**,
pp. 173–4

CAMBRIDGESHIRE
Josie and Jeff Harrison
Walnut Cottage
Winwick
Huntingdon PE17 5PP

DORSET
T. Parker (*fine Freesia sewing
   needles and threads*)
124 Corhampton Road
Boscombe East
Bournemouth BH6 5NZ

KENT
Denis Hornsby
25 Manwood Avenue
Canterbury CT2 7AH

LINCOLNSHIRE
Ken and Pat Schultz
Whynacres
Shepeau Stow
Whaplode Drove
Spalding PE12 0TU

MERSEYSIDE
Hayes & Finch
Head Office & Factory
Hanson Road
Aintree
Liverpool L9 9BP

NORTH HUMBERSIDE
Teazle Embroideries
35 Boothferry Road
Hull

NORTH YORKSHIRE
Stitchery
Finkle Street
Richmond

SOUTH YORKSHIRE
D.H. Shaw
47 Lamor Crescent
Thrushcroft
Rotherham S66 9QD

STAFFORDSHIRE
J. & J. Ford (*Dragonfly 140
   thread*)
October Hill
Upper Way
Upper Longdon
Rugeley WS15 1QB

SURREY
Needle and Thread
80 High Street
Horsell
Woking GU21 4SZ

SUSSEX
Southern Handicrafts
20 Kensington Gardens
Brighton BN1 4AC

Index

adding threads (Gros Point) 28
Aemelia Ars 110
Alençon 107–9
applied couronnes 35
applied petals 64
Argentan 106
attaching final row (Point de
    Gaze) 59

building up the trace (Gros
    Point) 27–8
buttonholed loops 29–32

circular samples (Hollie Point) 50
corded Brussels 13
cordonnet 18
cordonnette 24, 61
couching 18, 54
couronnes
    applied 35
    flower 39
    Point de Gaze 63, 89
    tiny 95
    threaded 36

Daisy wheels 81
decreasing 17
designing (Hollie Point) 50
diamonds
    four hole 14
    Gros Point 16
    nine hole 16
double Brussels 13

English stitch (Hollie Point) 40

fern leaves (Point de Gaze) 93–4
fil de trace 25
flower couronnes 39

Gibbons, Grinling 13, 38
grid fillings 98–102
ground (Point de Gaze) 59

Halas 133, 160

increasing 17
inverted pyramids 152

joining
    couronne 36
    new thread 46
    a ring 78

loops
    buttonholed 29
    trefoil 31–2
    zigzag 34

negotiating tight bends (Gros
    Point) 29

open veins 17, 58

padding threads 28
Pea stitch 13–14
Pea stitch variation 3a 129
picots
    looped 29–33
    Venetian 33
Point d'Espagne 41

raised spots (Point de Gaze) 71
raising (Gros Point) 25
Rosebud knots 71–2
Rosebud wheels 78

scalloped edge 88
scrolls 76–102
separate petals (Point de Gaze) 75
shading (Point de Gaze) 66
single buttonholed loops 29
spider web wheel 97
stitches
    corded Brussels 13

double Brussels 13
English stitch (Hollie Point) 40
Hollie stitch 42
inverted pyramids 152
Pea 13–14
Pea stitch variation 3a 129
picots (Venetian) 33
Point d'Espagne 41
stumpwork 10, 114, 146

tight bends (Gros Point) 29
tips
    Gros Point
        cordonnette 24–5
        couching 18, 20
        fillings 20–1
    Hollie Point
        before you start 44
    Point de Gaze
        before you start 54
    scrolls
        before you start 83
trace stitches (Gros Point) 25
trefoil loops 31–2
twisted bars (Point de Gaze) 60

veins 17
Venetian picots 33
vertical holes (Hollie Point) 50

wheels
    Daisy 81
    Rosebud knot 78
    spider web 97
    woven 60

Youghal 103

zigzag loops (Gros Point) 34